# WHEN IT WAS GREAT

*I hope you like all my true stories of Vegas.*

*Jim Sinatra*

# WHEN IT WAS GREAT

*The Old Vegas I Knew and Loved*

# Jim Sinay and Wid Bastian

Copyright © 2015 Jim Sinay

All rights reserved to the authors. No part of this publication may be reproduced in any form or by any means without the prior permission of the authors.

ISBN-13: 978-1530516292
ISBN-10: 1530516293

Website: whenitwasgreat.com
Twitter: www.twitter.com/whenitwasgreat
Facebook: www.facebook.com/whenitwasgreat
Gmail: whenitwasgreat1@gmail.com

# Contents

| | |
|---|---|
| Foreword | 1 |
| The Town | 6 |
| Welcome to Vegas, Jimmy | 13 |
| Let the Dealin' Begin | 21 |
| Onward and Upward | 27 |
| The Mint Gun Club | 33 |
| The Rat Pack, Johnny and Louis Prima | 38 |
| The Duke and Elvis | 45 |
| The Binions and the Italian Club | 51 |
| Femme Fatales | 60 |
| The Sahara | 72 |
| Takin' it a Bit Too Far | 81 |
| Mom Moves to Vegas | 89 |
| Cindy, the New York Jets and Pinky | 96 |

| | |
|---|---:|
| The Bachelor Book and the Great Chip Robbery | 104 |
| The Silverbird, Redd Foxx and Dancing with Debbie | 110 |
| It Wasn't All Fun and Games | 115 |
| Felicia Atkins and Showgirl Island | 125 |
| The Kinky Stuff | 130 |
| A Sporting Life | 143 |
| The Tropicana | 155 |
| Cheaters | 165 |
| Heading for the Exit | 171 |
| Jim's Acknowledgments | 182 |

# Foreword

I'm a big kid. Even though now I'm an old guy, seventy plus and looking at the back end of life, I'm still a kid at heart. My mother, God rest her sweet soul, called me "Big Dummy". She meant that with the upmost affection. I moved to Vegas in my early thirties and stayed there for three decades. I dealt casino games, craps mostly. I was a bachelor during those years. And a bit of a drinker. And a bit of carouser. Hey, I lived the high life back then. Those were my glory years. They were Vegas' glory years as well.

**Jimmy Today**

While I can honestly say that I never meant to harm another living soul, I know I didn't quite pull it off. Vegas was a party 24/7 and I took full advantage of it. But I always looked out for my friends and they always looked out for me. Did we invent a new wonder drug to cure a disease or save an endangered animal from extinction or build a better mousetrap? No, we didn't do that. We were in the entertainment business. Mostly we entertained ourselves and anyone we came in contact with.

Vegas in 2015, well, it's not for me. The Vegas I loved had a hundred thousand people living in it and hotels like the Dunes, the Sands, the El Rancho and the Horseshoe Club. While some of the old joints still exist, they are nothing like they used to be. Today Vegas is a giant adult Disneyland. People don't gamble, they go "gaming". No one dresses up to go a show anymore; people walk into the showrooms in blue jeans and tee shirts. Live music is hard to find – back in the day places like Caesars Palace had a live orchestra and headliners like Frank Sinatra and Tony Bennett. Nowadays you still have the superstars, but their names are Brittany Spears, Celine Dion, Shania Twain and Boys II Men. Not that they aren't fantastic, but the productions are huge and the music is from another generation.

If you walk down the Strip today, you won't get twenty yards until some yahoo hands you a flyer laced with pornography. I'm not a prude, as you'll soon discover by reading on, but I like to think I have some class. Prostitution has always been a part of Vegas and always will be. Only now it's done in the open for everyone to see. I don't want little kids seeing that crap. It didn't use to be that way.

When It Was Great, Vegas was a family friendly town. If your mother, sister, wife or girlfriend worked at a joint and she was harassed by some idiot or assaulted by a pervert, it was handled. You didn't call the cops, you told your boss at the casino and it was taken care of. Street crime was simply not tolerated, especially near the casinos. The Sheriff for almost all those years was a fella named Ralph Lamb. Sheriff Ralph was tight with "the boys", the guys who ran the joints, and things ran smoothly. Now, I know Vegas was smaller back then and things have changed and blah, blah, blah. All I'm saying is I liked it the way it used to be. There was a code, an ethic – don't lie, cheat or steal, mind your own business and have a good time. If you were stupid enough to try and steal from the casinos or mess with their employees, well, "ya got what was comin' to ya".

It's hard for anyone today to know what Vegas was really like decades ago. The films about the era do it some justice. For instance, I love *Casino* and I knew some of the real guys portrayed in that picture (read on for more on that), but the everyday Joe, like me, his story hasn't really been told. I dealt craps to celebs like John Wayne and Colonel Parker (Elvis' manager), but I didn't mingle with those guys. I'm a working man.

Back then everybody knew everybody else. The town was booming. New businesses sprang up like flowers after an April rain. In the 1970s the economy in Vegas was on a roll while the rest of America suffered through some stagnant times. Whether you worked in the casinos or you were a school teacher or a fireman or a restaurant owner, life was good. Damn good. Working stiffs like me bought houses and rented them out and eventually sold them and made a bunch of dough. The rising tide floated a lot of ships.

What's the worst thing that happened back in the day? From my point of view, it was when Wall Street discovered that "gaming" was a legitimate business. The mob had known that since forever, but it wasn't until the 1980s that corporate America discovered that, lo and behold, a casino was an incredibly profitable enterprise if it was run honestly and efficiently. What followed after that was a complete takeover and a brutal one. The real power, the big money guys in the world, American megacorps, muscled out the mob. Circus Circus went public in 1983 and then it was "Katy bar the door".

It was also the death knell for the Vegas I loved.

The late 1980s saw the beginning of the biggest boom in Vegas' history. Mega resorts were built, one after another. Once you could walk down the Strip and see open desert between resorts; now every square inch is packed - jammed with people, hucksters and riff raff of every kind. Ah, progress! I'm not always a fan of progress, but I'm certainly smart enough to know that what happened to Vegas was inevitable. Unfortunate, but inevitable.

I left Vegas in 2000. I retired at that time from the gambling business. I'd had enough and my mother needed me to help care for her back in Ohio. Now all I have are my memories. I'd like to share them with you. I hope my stories make you smile.

Like I said, I'm still a big kid, a well-meaning working stiff who likes to have a good time. Part of me will always be back in old Vegas, dealing craps at three in the morning and wondering if life would always be so good…

# The Town

In 1829 a Mexican scout by the name of Raphael Rivera was a member of a trading party headed towards Los Angeles from points east. In the nineteenth century, small parts of the Las Vegas Valley contained artesian wells that supported grass and trees. When Rivera saw these oases he called the valley Las Vegas, which means The Meadows in Spanish. A couple of decades later John C. Fremont passed through the Las Vegas Valley while it was still part of Mexico. Not long after that, Mexico ceded all of what is now Nevada to the United States after the Mexican American War.

William Bringhurst led a group of Mormon missionaries from Utah to the Las Vegas Valley in 1855. They built a small fort but abandoned it in 1857 after the summer heat proved too intense to grow crops. The U.S. Army reclaimed the old Mormon fort during the Civil War. After the war ended, the Feds made peace with the local Paiute tribe and a man named Octavius Glass started irrigating the old fields, growing grapes and making wine.

The fort/ranch changed hands several times until it was purchased by the San Pedro, Los Angeles and Salt Lake Railroad in 1902. Water from wells was piped into Las Vegas allowing for further growth. Once the railroad line was completed, Las Vegas was connected to the rest of America. On May 15, 1905 Las Vegas was officially founded as a city. On

October 1, 1910 the State of Nevada followed suit with the rest of the western states and outlawed gambling.

In July of 1930 President Herbert Hoover signed the appropriation bill for the Boulder Dam, which was to be built on the Colorado River just south of Vegas. Taking advantage of this temporary population and money influx, the Nevada Legislature approved legalized gambling. Las Vegas already had a small but well established illegal gambling industry. The Northern Club on Fremont Street was issued the first Nevada gambling license. From then until the Boulder Dam was completed in 1935, a steady stream of thousands of workers came from the dam site to Vegas to gamble and party.

When Boulder Dam started producing power, Vegas built "Glitter Gulch" on Fremont Street. The new electricity flow supported thousands of bright lights. In 1940 Route 95 opened, giving the city two major access roads. During the Second World War, the Army built a gunnery school for its pilots in the Vegas Valley. This school would later become Nellis Air Force Base. More clubs were built and the town expanded.

In 1946 mobster Bugsy Siegel, with help from his pal Meyer Lansky, built the first true resort hotel in Vegas, The Flamingo. Siegel was murdered in Beverly Hills in 1947, but his vision for Vegas lived on. In the 1950s more mob money built more resorts, along with help from Mormon bankers to give everything a thin cloak of legitimacy. The Sahara, Sands, New Frontier, Royal Nevada, Showboat, Riviera, Fremont, Tropicana and Binion's Horseshoe came into being. Modern Vegas was born.

Everyone knew that gangsters were building and operating the hotels. However, money talked and everything else walked. By 1954 over 8

million people were visiting Vegas pumping $200 million dollars into the casinos. The Feds tried to spoil the Vegas party during the famous Kefauver Committee hearings. There was no doubt that organized crime was controlling the casinos, but nevertheless Nevada Senator Pat McCarran was able to stop a proposal for the Feds to regulate gambling on a national basis. For a time, the mob was safe and Vegas just kept rolling along.

Howard Hughes came to Vegas in 1966. He stayed at the Desert Inn and decided that he didn't want to leave. Rather than being evicted, he bought the hotel. He kept on buying too; more hotels, real estate and media outlets. Hughes added more money and mystique to the ever growing Las Vegas "Miracle in the Desert".

There were scandals and setbacks, players and wanna bes that came and went, but Vegas kept expanding. Every decade the population of the city doubled. By 1968 the joints were hopping, the money was flowing and life was good.

That's when I arrived….

After I finished high school in 1956, I went to college for a year. I wanted to see and be somewhere else so I quit school and went to Florida. I worked as a port diver cleaning ships and then as a lifeguard. After a while I came home because the jobs were few down South at the time. Ohio wasn't much better employment wise so I joined the Navy.

I went overseas to Vietnam and saw parts of China, the Philippines and Japan. I played basketball for the All-Navy team. In sum, it was a great experience. After four years I came home and Mom and Dad welcomed me with open arms like they always did.

Jimmy in the Navy in 1961

As a seaman, I spent some time in California. So I decided to go see what kinda money I could make out there. I worked as a bartender for a bit and then as a car repo man for a detective agency. That was unpleasant. I found that people didn't like me taking their rides from them. I had guns pulled on me, knives too so I said to myself, "This is stupid." I got my butt outta there and went back to Ohio.

I wasn't a kid anymore, I was lookin' at thirty. It was time to do something more substantial with my life, so I got a job at Republic Steel. In the late 1960s jobs at steel companies were great jobs with good pay and benefits. I quickly rose up the ranks to become a foreman. In '68, Republic had a big layoff. They had to get rid of four foremen and I was one of them.

As I always did, I turned to Mom and Dad for advice. I told them that I had no idea what to do now. So far, everything I'd tried career wise simply had not worked out. Mom thought I should go back to school, get my degree and get into coaching and teaching. I'd always wanted to do that. It sounded like a good idea.

When I'm faced with a big decision, I like to think it over. So that night I went to downtown Canton and had a drink. I was in this bar I'd been in many times before and in walked a very familiar face. I called him Uncle Ed. His name was Ed Pucci. He was Frank Sinatra's bodyguard and a local legend. Since I was a little boy, I always called him Uncle Ed. His sister and my mother used to hang out and I grew up watching Uncle Ed play football.

**Ed Pucci 1948**

We started talking. Uncle Ed asked me what was going on and I told him – I'd lost my job at the steel mill and didn't really know what to do next. I told him that I might go back to college and finish my degree. I didn't have any money so I had to get a job.

"Why don't you go out to Vegas?" Uncle Ed asked me.

"Vegas?" I said. "What would I do out there?"

"Be a dealer," Uncle Ed said.

"I don't know nothin' about that," I said.

"What's to know?" Uncle Ed explained. "You go to school and you learn. If you're interested, you let me know. I can help you out."

I talked to Mom and Dad about what Uncle Ed and I discussed. Mom said to me, "Jimmy, you Big Dummy, until you figure out what you want to do in life you'll never be settled and happy. You went to Florida, joined the Navy and then went back to California. None of that was for you. You'll always have a home to come back to here."

"Whaddya think Mom?" I asked.

"Give Vegas a try. Give it a year, year and a half. If you don't like it, come back to Ohio," Mom said. "You can always go back to Kent State, get your degree then you can go coach and teach."

I was blessed to have two great parents. They gave me the freedom and the security to find myself. I loved them dearly, I still do.

In November of 1968 I paid off all my bills and said my goodbyes. Uncle Ed told me who to go see out in Vegas about a dealer job. I hopped in my '64 Green Caddy convertible and left. I had no idea what might happen next. Vegas was nothing to me but a dot on the map and a place I'd heard about on TV.

# Welcome to Vegas, Jimmy

There was a family friend out in Vegas who I'd called in advance. She told me that I could come and stay with her for a day or two and she would show me around town. So that's what I did. The day after I arrived we got in my car and drove around town. Vegas was a really nice place, not too big, and to me it was full of wonders. Back then, the Strip and Fremont Street were something to behold. I loved the lights and all the excitement. Since it was November, it wasn't too hot. I was looking forward to a pleasant winter, like the ones I'd enjoyed in Florida.

The next day my friend introduced me to a lady she knew who rented out rooms for $25 a month. She had a four bedroom place over off of Charleston. This gal looked like Ethel Norton from the *Honeymooners*. Pleasant lady, but not overly friendly. She showed me the bedroom. It was nice enough. Then "Ethel" told me the rules.

"You eat anything out of the refrigerator make sure it's your own. No bringing women over to the house and when my dog needs to go outside let her out and be sure to bring her back in."

"Got it," I said. Didn't seem like any big deal to me. I could live with those rules. So I rented the room.

Her other two rooms were also rented out to young guys. I briefly introduced myself to them and turned in for the night.

The next day I got up and went to the Stardust casino. Uncle Ed told me to go there and see a man by the name of Al Sachs. Al was a distinguished looking guy, in an Italian sorta way. He dressed nice, but not like he was going to church. This man ran a casino, not an Elks Club, and he looked the part big time. He had a definite air of importance about him, but he wasn't cocky. Back then I didn't really know what a big shot Al was, but as the General Manager of the Stardust Al Sachs was an important person in Vegas.

I was Jimmy Sinay from Canton. A nobody. I showed up and sat down in the waiting area. A minute or two later the secretary showed me into his office.

"Can I help you?" Al Sachs asked me.

"I'm Jim Sinay. I'm here looking for a job."

"What kinda job are you looking for?" Al asked me.

"A dealer job."

"Where have you dealt?" Sachs asked.

"I've never dealt anywhere. I'm new in town and I'm lookin' to become a dealer."

Al smiled, chuckled and then said, "Look young man. In order to be a dealer, you have to go to school. You do all that downtown. Then you work downtown for a year or two until you get the games down. When you think you're good enough you come out on the Strip and you audition at a place that has openings for dealers."

Al stuck out his hand and said, "I wanna wish you luck."

I said, "Thank you, sir. The only reason I came to see you was because my Uncle Ed Pucci said I should talk to you about a dealing job."

Al's expression suddenly got a bit more serious. "Sit back down. How do you spell your last name?"

"S…i…n…a…y."

Al left me sitting in his office. He went into the other room and closed the door. Fifteen minutes later he re-appeared. Al walked up to me and said, "Here." He handed me a piece of paper. "Go down to the Fremont Hotel. Go see a man by the name of Al Bayless. He's waiting for ya. You'll learn craps, blackjack and roulette. You'll work downtown as a shill for nine dollars. After a year or so, when you think you're good enough, I'll give you an audition and if you pass I'll put you to work."

We shook hands. I left and drove down to the Fremont Hotel. I found Al Bayless without any trouble. He'd been waiting for me. We walked back to his office and I sat down across from him.

"You need to go down to the Sherriff's office and get a Sheriff's Work Card," Bayless told me. "That'll give you permission to work in a casino. Everyone has to have a Sheriff's card. You'll come to the school between ten in the morning and noon. We'll teach you the games. We're gonna put you to work as a shill, between ten at night and four in the morning."

"Okay," I said. "That sounds good. Nine dollars an hour, that's not too bad."

"Where'd you get nine dollars an hour?" Bayless asked me.

I said, "Mr. Sachs said I'd make nine dollars."

He said, "That's right. You'll make nine dollars for the six to eight hour shift depending on how long we need ya."

"Nine dollars for the whole shift?" I asked.

"Yes," he said. "And it costs $25 a week to go to school here. We will take that out of your paycheck every two weeks."

"Okay… What's a shill?" I asked.

"A shill is a man who is called to a game by the house. We give him checks and he plays until the game starts to fill up. Once the game gets going, the shill hands his checks back in and stands where we can find him. A lot of customers don't want to go to an empty game," Bayless explained.

"Got it," I said.

Nine dollars a night? Hard to live on that wage, I said to myself. But that's the way it was, that was the deal. Prove yourself first, get paid later.

When I went back home, I found out that my two other roommates were also working at the Fremont as shills. That was kinda nice. The three of us went to school at the same time and then pulled the night shift as shills.

The Fremont was a joint that catered to working people on vacation or locals. Very few, if any, high rollers frequented the place. The food was decent, the rooms were clean and the casino was friendly. The stakes were generally low on most of the tables.

On our first day at the Fremont as novice dealers, the instructor explained the basics to us. "Number one," the instructor said as he held up a stack of what I always thought were chips, "these are not called chips. They're called checks. Number two, when you're on a game and you're leaving it you will clean your hands." He showed us how to do this by clapping his hands together and displaying empty palms. "Number three, on a craps table, and that's the game you'll be learning first, you gotta learn the terminology."

So the man went through the basics of craps. He showed us how to call out the bets, how to call the dice and so on. This took him about 45

minutes or so. Then we learned some things about blackjack and roulette. When the day's lesson was over the instructor gave each of us a stack of checks from a casino that had closed. The checks were worthless except as teaching tools. He said that we had to practice cutting and sizing these checks over and over until we became proficient at the art.

"How does all this work?" I asked.

"Let's say you have a payoff of five dollars. The white checks are a dollar. Instead of giving the guy one red, five dollar check, you'll stack the same number of white checks he has on the table and size 'em so he's been paid five dollars. That's called sizing." Then the instructor demonstrated how to size a stack of checks.

"Use your forefinger to cut checks from the stack in your hand and place them on the table to pay off a bet. If I'm paying off a forty dollar bet, then I'll cut eight red checks from the stack and slide them off to the player." Then the man demonstrated this technique.

All of this sounds so simple. But when you're dealing a fast paced game, whether its craps, roulette or blackjack, you have to do all this automatically. I suppose it requires a certain amount of basic math skill, but more spatial than math skill is required; so many white, red, green or black checks, etc. When you're dealing, you don't even think in terms of money unless a customer puts down a bill and asks to purchase checks.

The next day, the instructor got specific about how we need to call the dice at the craps table. We stood around the table where bettors would stand and the instructor handed the dice to one of the students.

"Let me show you fellas how this works," the instructor said. "Alright get your bets down. How much goes." Then he motioned for the student to throw the dice. When the dice hit the wall on the other end and came

to rest, the instructor said, "Six. Came out at six, the point's six. How much on the hard ways." He kept on barking "How much" on this and that.

Then he gave the dice back to the shooter and said, "Point six, point six." The shooter rolled again. "Nine, centerfield nine." Then the instructor stopped and said, "Gentlemen, remember to look in the field. See what numbers are there – 2, 3, 4, 9, 10, 11 and 12. In a game five and nine sound very similar and it can be hard to hear because people are screaming and hollering at times. So when nine is rolled you say 'Nine, field roll nine'. If they roll a five you say, 'Five, no field five'. The dealers on the other side of the table need to hear you clearly. On the come out roll, if it comes out seven you say 'Winner seven, front line winner seven'. If it comes out eleven you say, "Yo eleven, front line winner eleven.'"

"Can't the dealers on the other end just watch the dice and see what number is thrown?" a student asked.

"If you're on the other end of the table you do not watch the dice. Never, I repeat never, take your eyes off of the checks. You protect your end." Turning his attention to the student who asked him the question, the instructor asked, "What's the three most important words in real estate?"

"Uh…," the student hesitated. "Location, location, location?"

"That's right," the instructor said. "What's the three most important words in a casino?"

No one had an answer. After a moment the instructor said, "Protect the money, protect the money and protect the money."

After a week or so we all knew what rule number one was and that it was never to be violated – protect the house's money. If you can't do that, you don't deserve to be working.

Training at the tables during the day was only half of the program. Being a shill was the other part of the deal. I went to work dressed in black pants and a long sleeved white shirt, exactly how they wanted us dressed. In those days, that's what dealers wore at most of the joints.

After I'd been a shill for a while, maybe a couple of weeks or so, one night I was standing with the guys off to the side, ten to fifteen feet away from the game. We were watching a twenty one game that night. It was about midnight, as I recall, and it was the dealer's turn for a break. The next dealer came in, tapped him on the shoulder and the dealer set the cards down. He cleaned his hands and took a step away from the table.

The dealer took another couple of steps away from the game and out of the bottom of his pants rolled a $25 check. The guy froze. He looked down at the check. I looked at it. The pit boss, the man in charge, had his

arms folded in front of his chest. He bent over and he saw the check. The dealer took another step and another check fell out.

I didn't say a word, didn't have to. Anyone watching could figure out what was going down. The dealer looked around and saw the pit boss staring at him. So the dealer took off his apron, threw it on the floor and said, "I quit". Then he headed for the exit.

Every other step the guy took another $25 check fell out of his pants. The dealer was wearing what we called a sub, a tube made of cloth that goes down the inside of a pant leg from the belt down to the knee. The sub is wide enough to slip a check inside it when someone's not looking. That's why you never touch your belt or pockets while you're working.

The dealer made it out the door. The pit boss just watched the whole thing and didn't say a word. I never heard what happened to the thief.

I can tell you this – back in the 60s, 70s and early 80s if you stole from the casino sometimes you disappeared and were never heard from again. Sometimes a thief might wake up with a broken hand so he couldn't deal anymore. If you were lucky, you left town on your own and if you weren't too big of a fish no one came after you.

What happened to thieves was none of my business. The boys who ran the casinos didn't call the cops and file a theft report, that's for sure. They dealt with problems swiftly and, in my view, fairly. Say what you want about it, but that's the way it was.

For honest guys like me, I never had to worry about making the wrong people mad. But if you had sticky fingers… Remember the scene in *Casino* where Joe Pesci's character goes after a cheat with a hammer in the back room of the joint? That type of thing really happened and not just once in a while. It was the way things were done.

# Let the Dealin' Begin

I got out of dealer's school in early 1969. By the time I was ready to go to work I also got my own place, an apartment at the Patrician Arms on 551 East Desert Inn Road. This was a wonderful complex where I lived for over twenty years. The bottom floor was all studio or one bedroom apartments. The top two floors were two bedroom units – kitchen and dining room on the second floor, bedrooms on the third floor.

**Jimmy In Front Of The Patrician Arms**

My apartment looked out at Desert Inn Road. You could see the Hilton and Landmark hotels from my balcony. Probably the best part about the Patrician Arms was that everyone, and I mean everyone, that lived there was single and between the ages of 21 and 50. If you wanted to meet a nice girl, all ya had to do was grab your towel and head down to the pool.

My first roommate was a guy named Bruce King. His nickname was Boogaloo. There was a dance called Boogaloo back in those days and Bruce loved to Boogaloo whenever he could. Boog and I hung out together and went on double dates. He was a great guy.

My first job was dealing at the Carousel downtown. It was a small club – two craps tables, maybe eight blackjack tables, a bar and a modest restaurant. Most of us working there were "breaking in" dealers, greenhorns if you will. The rest of the guys were either old fellas whose best days were behind them or people who had a background problem of some sort and couldn't work on the Strip. We were paid $12.50 per day plus tips. Only we didn't call them tips, we called them tokes. In 1969, my tokes ran anywhere from six bucks to maybe once in a while getting $25 to $35 a shift. I wasn't gettin' rich back then, but I was having a hell of a good time.

I made friends fast, I always do. One of my buddies was Ron. He was a craps dealer like me. The boss closed a game down one morning (it was around four a.m.) because there wasn't enough customers and the table needed to be cleaned. So Ron took a double break. On his breaks, Ron would go across the street to the Vegas Club or the Golden Gate and he'd get a drink or two. Or three, or… you get the picture.

About 45 minutes after Ron left he had still had not returned. His double break was only 40 minutes. We'd started the game back up again.

Ron appeared a moment later and tapped the guy on the back and took over the stick.

The pit boss said to Ron, "Where were you?"

"I made a mistake," Ron said sheepishly.

"What happened?" I asked.

"I got through drinking and I walked into the Golden Gate. I tapped the stick guy on the shoulder and he pointed to the shooter. I called the dice for about three minutes. I looked around and didn't recognize anybody. I noticed that they didn't have any Carousel shirts on.

"I looked at the boss and said, 'Isn't this the Carousel?' He said, 'No, it's the Golden Gate'. I said, 'I'm sorry. I'm in the wrong joint!' I set the stick down, cleaned my hands turned around and walked out. Then I came back over here."

Everyone at the table had a good laugh. It was funny and Ron told the story so matter of fact - like it was no big deal that he just started dealing craps in a casino he didn't work in.

That sort of thing was fairly common. On breaks guys drank. Today you'd get fired on the spot for doing something like that as a craps dealer in a Vegas casino. Back in the day we took it in stride. Alcohol and Vegas went together like hand in glove. I really can't imagine one without the other.

Maybe we weren't so serious back then. We didn't take ourselves seriously, that's for sure, but we had to take our job seriously. While the boys could care less if we drank on the job, we had to do our job right or we'd soon find ourselves unemployed (or worse). But back then it was gambling, not gaming. People gambled to have a good time and let loose. That attitude definitely spilled over to the dealers.

Three of the guys, myself included, who went to work at the Carousel after going to school at the Fremont kept our stack of checks that were given to us for training. They weren't worth anything, the casino that issued them was long closed, but we practiced our cuts and slices with them when we went out for a beer or were just hanging out.

One night the three of us went down to this bar on Boulder Highway. I've got these checks and I'm cutting them on the bar. We were doing "somethin' close to nothin'" as the old saw goes. In walks this beautiful woman. She was maybe 25 or so. She sat on a bar stool ten feet away from me. My buddies and I all noticed her and we whispered to each other how gorgeous she was.

Wouldn't you know it, a few seconds later she smiled at me and said, "Can I come over and join ya?"

"Sure, come on," I said. I told the bartender to give her a drink.

I asked what her name was and she said, "Ginger." I introduced her to my two buddies.

"Whaddya do?" I asked her.

She said, "I'm a working girl."

"Where do you work?" I asked innocently enough.

She just smiled and said, "I'm a working girl."

In Vegas back in the day a "working girl" was a hooker, a prostitute. Me, being the dummy I was, did not know this.

My buddy next to me said, "Jim, she's a hooker."

I leaned over to Ginger, which by now even a dummy like me had figured out was not her real name and said, "I'm sorry. I'm new to Vegas."

"That's okay," Ginger said. "I just wondered if you boys were interested or not."

I said, "I don't know." I turned and talked to my buddies and asked them. They just nodded and smiled.

So I looked at Ginger and asked, "How much?"

Ginger looked us over and replied, "For all three of ya? A hundred and twenty dollars."

I was still cutting my training checks out on the bar. So I said to the beautiful Ginger, "Would you take these checks?"

She looked at my stack of $25 checks and she said, "Sure."

So we went down to this dive motel where she was staying - there were a bunch of these seedy little places near Fremont Street in 1970. Each of us took our turn, one at a time. At the end of it I looked at Ginger, she was sitting there in a robe with nothin' on underneath, and I said, "You know what? You were so good and you're such a nice person I'm gonna give you $200 in checks." So I cut out eight of the worthless, green $25 checks and gave them to her.

She looked at me and said, "Thank you so much. I'm a teacher in California and I'm trying to put enough money together to get my Master's degree."

I said, "Okay honey. Good luck."

The three of us got in the car as fast as we could and took off. I always suspected, maybe feared is a better word, that Ginger went around town looking for us. We never ran into her, that's for sure. But then again maybe she just laughed it off and chalked it up to experience. The odds of her

being a "teacher from California trying to get a Master's degree" were about as good as her being able to cash in those checks.

That kind of thing happened all the time, the crazy fooling around antics. Grown men acting like fifteen year olds.

God help me, I loved those days. I didn't have a care in the world.

# Onward and Upward

When my dealing skills improved, I migrated from the Carousel Club to the Mint Hotel. I made a whopping $17.50 a day at the Mint. Of course, dealers make their money from tokes, not salary. The tokes were a little better at the Mint, but I was by no means getting rich. I had to find creative ways to stretch a buck.

One of the things I would do is go to the Circus Circus Hotel and chow down at their buffet. Back then, it cost 99 cents for all you could eat. The food was more than decent and I always filled my belly. I also filled bags that were in my pockets with more food and brought it home for my roommate and me to eat later.

In the old Vegas, and in the new to a lesser degree, a guy could eat well for very little money. The Circus Circus buffet had the best combination of quality and value, but other joints also put out top class spreads for a small charge. That was part of the marketing equation of the old casinos – practically give away the food, the booze and even the rooms and make your money on the gambling. Now days every portion of a "resort" is a profit center – the rooms, the food, the parking even the alcohol is priced to make money.

When I first started at the Mint, since I was the new guy, I was regularly assigned to what we called the "Bird Game". The Bird Game is when you have 25 cent checks on the layout – in other words there isn't a lot of

money being wagered. A lot of people liked the Bird Game because they could play for hours and not risk much dough – maximum entertainment, minimum risk.

The first week I was working at the Mint a guy named Lefty McEdwards was supervising a Bird Game I was dealing. At the Carousel we never had a large number of players around the table, but at the Mint it was different, especially at the Bird Game. For the first time I had seven or eight players on my end. I made one mistake after another. I was completely frazzled by all the action! I made the wrong payoffs. I lost track of what was going on. In sum, I really screwed things up.

Lefty, God bless him, was very patient. He called out the corrections saying things like, "You gave him two dollars too much" or "Add three dollars to that stack" and so on. After the game slowed down and almost all the players left, Lefty stood up, walked next to me and said, "Hey kid. I don't know what you're on, but I'd like to have some of that stuff for later on."

I wanted to crawl away and die I was so embarrassed. I said, "Lefty, I don't do drugs. Haven't been drinkin' either."

"I know that," Lefty said with a big grin on his face. "I'm bustin' your chops. Don't worry about a thing. I'm here, I'll protect ya. Just remember – do it correctly, the way you were taught and you'll be fine."

That word of encouragement was all I needed. I took a few deep breaths and things went a lot better from that time on. It wasn't easy breaking in. Everything seems so simple when you learn it. If there are only a few players around the table it's pretty easy to follow the action. But when you get twenty people all crowding around a craps table and they are

yelling and screaming and reaching across the table to place and pick up bets, it's suddenly not so simple anymore.

Still a relatively new dealer at the Mint, I was on the base one day when this blind man came in. I'd noticed this blind guy before standing outside the Mint and Horseshoe before asking for money. Now I guess he had enough dough to try his luck at the table.

The blind man came up to my side of the table, put his cane down and handed me a ten dollar bill.

"Please," the blind man said, "Give me five dollars in one dollar chips and five dollars in 25 cent chips."

I said, "Yes sir," and did as I was asked.

Then the blind guy said, "Put the 25 cent checks in the front rail and the dollar checks in the back rail, that way I'll know how to tell the difference between 'em."

"Okay sir," I said.

This blind gentleman liked to play the hard way bets – that's double twos for a four, double threes for a six, double fours for an eight and double fives for a ten. These bets pay different odds. In order to win your bet, the shooter must roll the number the hard way before he "craps out", rolls a seven.

You can either have the bets working on the come out roll, the first roll a new shooter makes, or you call the bets off on the come out roll. If the shooter rolls a seven on the come out roll and your hard way bet is on, you lose your hard way bet. If he rolls a soft way number on the come out roll you lose your hard way bet. If he rolls a hard way on the come out roll you win. I heard the blind man call off the hard way bets on the come out roll.

The stick man at the table was relieved right before the shooter took the dice to roll again. The stick man calls the dice in a crap game. The shooter rolled and the dice came up seven so the stick man said, "Seven, front line winner seven." The stick man reached over to grab the hard way bets the blind man had placed, not knowing that those bets were off – that the blind man could not win or lose on the first roll.

As soon as the stick man touched the blind guy's bets, the blind guy shouted, "Hey, I said my hard ways were off!"

I looked at the blind guy and said, "Sir. How did you know he was going to pick them up? I was just going to tell him to leave the bets on the table."

The blind guy stuttered and said, "I… uh… had this strong feeling, intuition… that he was going to take my bets."

I looked at the "blind" guy and said, "Don't bullshit a bullshitter, pal. I think you ought to find another game."

The "blind" guy collected his checks and moved on. I laughed about it. Just another Vegas story, the blind guy who can magically see his chips on the table…

There was another guy who hung out on the corner of Flamingo and Las Vegas Boulevard. I remember him well. He wore rags and looked like he hadn't had a bath in a month. He had a hand painted sign that read, "Out of work. Need money for food." As it turns out, that fella was making $20 an hour begging on that corner. In the 70s that was good money.

Vegas is one giant hustle. It still is, I'm sure, that much will never change. There are a ton of ways to make money and many of them are dishonest. Lying and scheming, that never sat well with me. Now, I'm

no saint that's for sure. I guess it comes down to self-respect. I wasn't raised to take advantage of anyone. That has always seemed to me to be a shameful way to conduct yourself.

Anyway…

After a while I got a new roommate, Don Knight. We were always screwing around with each other, pulling jokes. We liked to sit around the house and watch TV when we were off. So one night ol' Don and I were hanging out watching some ball game on TV and I went to get a frozen dinner from the fridge. I popped the thing in the oven and took it out when it was cooked. I sat down next to Don on the couch, put my dinner on the TV tray and opened the thing up.

Inside the foil was a potato skin. No potato, no entrée, just the skin. I didn't seem to me like the foil had been taken from the dinner, it looked like it just came that way from the store. I'd been ripped off.

I said, "Hey! Look at this! They sold me this TV dinner with only a lousy potato skin in it."

Don said, "Hey Jim. Take it back. How can they do something like that? That's just wrong."

As I was cursing the grocer and putting the TV dinner in a bag to take it back to the store, Don couldn't hold it in anymore and burst out laughing. He thought that was the funniest joke ever pulled. Shows you just how naïve I was back in those days…

I was dealing craps one night and it was slow, really slow. This happened from time to time. If there was no action, the dealers just stood around telling stories and laughing. We had to stay on the game for our shift even if there weren't any players.

My friend Johnny and I were yuking it up when an older guy, maybe seventy or so, walked up to our table. We stopped laughing and got ready to deal. The old guy tossed me a few bills and I handed him some checks. The dice were put in front of him on the table so he could pick two and start shootin'.

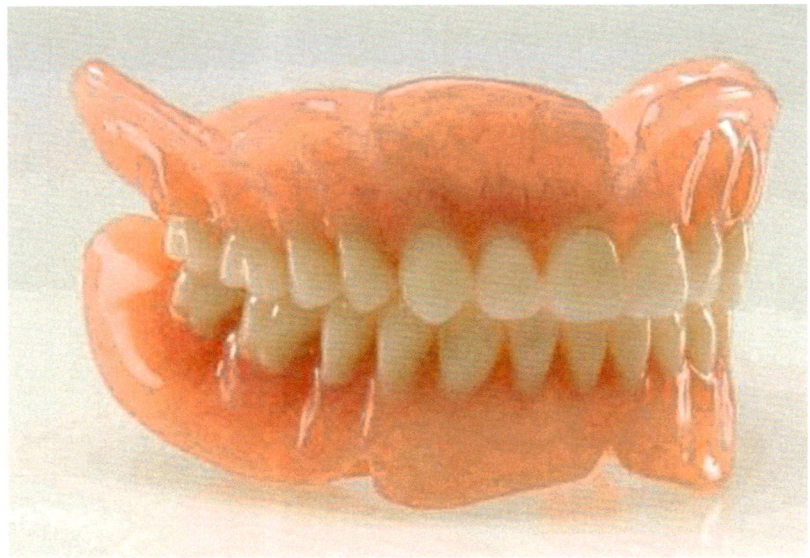

Well, when this old guy leaned over to pick his dice, his false teeth fell out right on the table. None of us were expecting that! I somehow (still not sure how) resisted the urge to bust out laughing. My buddy Johnny, who was dealing with me, reached into his mouth, pulled out his false teeth and tossed them on the table.

"You're faded, sir," Johnny said, meaning his bet was covered.

Now everybody just lost it. There weren't many people in the casino at the time, but the entire joint heard us all laugh. The old man and Johnny picked up their teeth and we rolled the dice.

# The Mint Gun Club

If you've seen the movie *Casino* that's really what it was like in Vegas back in the day. The real life counterpart of Robert DeNiro's character Sam Rothstein was a guy named Frank "Lefty" Rosenthal who ran four joints for the Chicago boys – the Stardust, the Hacienda, the Fremont and the Marina.

Back then all of the hotel casinos were financed by the mob, one way or another. The Teamsters Pension Fund was the biggest mob casino financing conduit. Now, you're gonna hear me say a lot of nice things about how the boys ran Vegas. Don't misunderstand me – in no way do I think that organized criminals are the kinda people I'd hold up as good people. I don't think murder and extortion and corruption are anything other than crimes.

But what I do want to convey is that for the average working guy like me and I'd say for the average resident of Vegas back then, the way the boys ran the town simply worked well for almost everyone.

If you lived in Vegas back in the 60s, 70s and early 80s then you know what I'm talking about. The boys were not interested in bothering anyone not associated with their businesses. They bought houses and lived in communities – in many ways they were like everybody else. The vast majority of the boys were not crazy animals like the Nicky Santoro character in *Casino*. Joe Pesci's portrayal of the real life Anthony Spilotro

was amazing and Spilotro was as crazy as Pesci portrayed him, but Spilotro was the exception, not the rule.

One day before going into work at the Mint I got a phone call from the boss, Paul. He told me that I was to report to the Mint Gun Club that night and not to the hotel. Why? I asked him. There was a game out there he needed me to deal, that's all he would say.

That's all he needed to say.

The Mint Gun Club was way out in the desert, in the middle of no man's land north of Vegas. You could shoot off cannons there all day long and not hit a building or any living creature. It was completely isolated. You could see anything coming at the place for miles in every direction.

When I got out there three other dealers and two bosses were waiting for me. We brought in the checks from the casino and set them up on a craps table. We no sooner got the table set up when the door on my right opened up. The room was maybe thirty feet long and thirty feet wide. In walked this guy with sunglasses on. He walked to the only other door to the room, opened it up and looked outside. Then he opened the door he originally came through and motioned with his hand, signaling to someone that it was okay to come in.

Twelve guys strolled in. They got around our table. The guy next to me asked for $5000 in checks. I cut them out for him. Then the boss starting putting "Lammers" on the table. A Lammer is a small plastic button with a number written on it – 1, 5, 10 or 20. Each Lammer represents thousands of dollars in credit. So if a guy had a Lammer with a ten written on it in front of him, that meant the house had given him $10,000 in credit.

The game started and the boys were all smoking and drinking and playing. I knew who I was in the room with – guys who could not come to Vegas and play openly in the casino. These fellas were blacklisted or at least most of them were.

If you were blacklisted by Nevada Gaming that meant that you were not allowed in any casino at any time or you were subject to immediate arrest. The only way you got blacklisted back then was if you were a notorious gangster or if you'd been caught cheating in the casino. None of these guys had ever been caught cheating in a Nevada casino. All of their last names ended in vowels. You get the picture.

The man next to me was laying thousands of dollars in bets. He liked to place odds on his pass line bets. Putting odds on the pass line bet increases the bet and is a smart move if you are playing with the shooter. I noticed that the gentleman had placed the wrong amount of money behind his bet, too much money.

The man was talking to his buddy so I leaned over to him and said, "Sir, your odds bet is not correct. You've put down too much money."

Standing right behind this man was his body guard. The next thing I know a giant hand is gently pushing me away from the man I was speaking to. The man looked back at his bodyguard and said, "That's okay." The man took his hand off of my chest.

"What's wrong with my bet?" the man asked me.

"You've got too much down, sir."

"Correct it for me."

So I fixed it and put the excess on the rail for him.

Two hours later they were done playing. The guy next to me says, "You did a great job young man," and he threw me $500 in checks. All of the

other guys all threw money in for the dealers. We each made several hundred bucks. A really good day for me.

The boys left as they came in – after the bodyguard made sure that the coast was clear they piled into several vehicles and took off. None of us in the building looked outside to see what they were driving.

After the boys were gone, my boss talked to me as we were securing the checks for transport back to the Mint.

"Hey Jimmy," my boss said to me, "do you know who that was standing next to you?"

I said, "Paul, I don't want to know, I don't care to know."

Paul smiled and said, "Jimmy, you were never here and this game never happened."

"Of course," I said. That much was a given.

Paul walked off. I put the chips away, did my job and drove back to Vegas.

I've become familiar with some of the blacklisted people back in the day through news media reports. I could tell you with a great deal of certainty who some of those boys were but even now, decades later, I know it's best to keep my mouth shut. The truth is all of those boys were always great to me and every other working stiff at the casino. Whatever else they did was none of my business.

# The Rat Pack, Johnny and Louis Prima

I was getting ready to go to work one afternoon at the Sahara Hotel when my Uncle Ed called me.

"Hey Jimmy," Ed said.

"Hey Ed. How are ya?" I said.

"Whaddya doin' after work tonight?" Ed asked.

"Not much. What's up?"

"Come on over to the Sands. Just tell the front desk I invited you up to a party. They'll tell ya where ya need to go," Ed explained.

"I'll be there," I said.

If Uncle Ed invited me to a party, I knew it had to be something special. His boss, Frank Sinatra, might be involved and maybe a few of Frank's friends. Unless I was dead I was goin'.

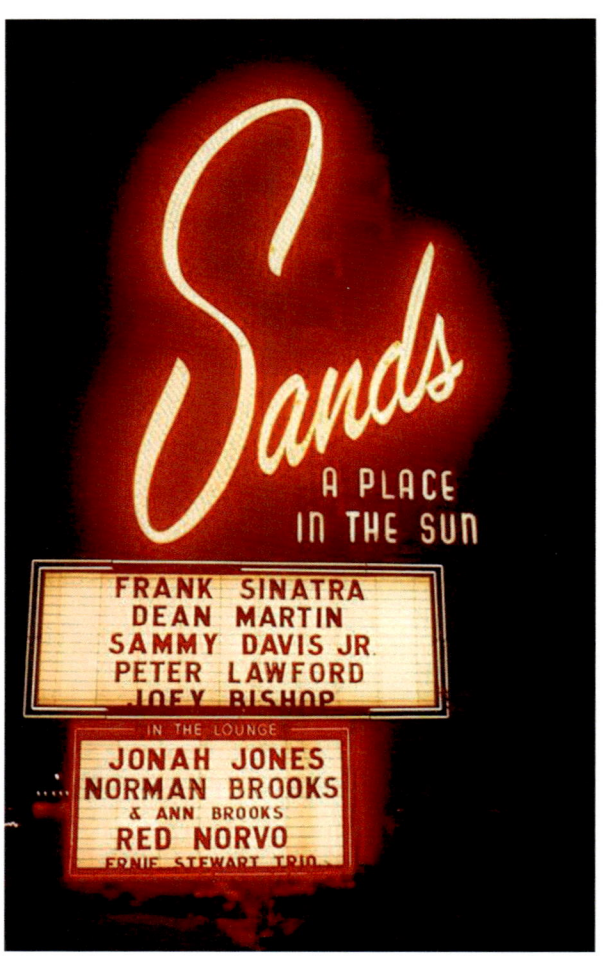

So that night after work I drove over to the Sands. I told the guy manning the elevator that Ed Pucci had invited me to a party. He hit the right button and up I went.

At the door another guy asked me who I was and I told him. He checked my name off of some list and let me in the suite.

The room was packed. Uncle Ed was there as was Frank Sinatra, Dean Martin, Sammy Davis, Jr., Joey Bishop, a lot of pretty girls (some showgirls with their make-up still on) and a bunch of other guys.

This was the first time I met Frank Sinatra. Ed introduced me and Frank and I talked for a little bit. I was kinda star struck, as you might imagine, but Frank was very polite. He treated me like one of the boys. I said hello to Dean Martin and talked with him for a few minutes too. What a thrill.

Sammy Davis, Jr. I'd met before. A year or so earlier, as I recall, I ran into Sammy in the grocery store. He had a huge bodyguard with him. This fella was gigantic!

I went up to Sammy and his massive guard and said, "Sammy Davis."

"Yes," he said.

"I think you know my Uncle," I said.

"Who is that?" Sammy said.

"Ed Pucci," I said.

"Oh yeah!" Sammy said, now comfortable. "I love Eddie. He's a great guy."

Sammy smiled, we talked. We swapped Ed Pucci stories. Sammy asked me if I'd seen any of his shows and I told him I caught a few but that I worked swing shifts as a dealer and so it was tough to go to shows.

When I saw Sammy again we got re-acquainted. The most striking thing about Sammy was his size. He was a little guy, maybe 5'6" or 5'7" and the man couldn't have weighed more than a buck thirty. When he smiled that magnificent smile of his, that's all you saw. He was one of a kind.

I had a great time. I met some beautiful women, had a few drinks and was generally lovin' life. Then I heard some commotion over in the corner. A lot of laughter and then some loud voices. Uncle Ed appeared from the crowd and took me aside for a private chat.

"Jimmy, if Frank gets upset about something, that's your cue to leave. There is absolutely no talkin' to Frank when he's hot. It's got nothin' to do with you personally. Just a heads up, Jimmy. Frank has a bad temper."

"Okay," I said to Ed. "I'll do that."

I stuck around a little longer and did my best to make some headway with the ladies. Frank didn't go off that night, but on another occasion when I was at one of the parties he did get upset. Uncle Ed didn't have to remind me what to do – as soon as Frank got mad (not at me, of course) I hit the door.

Celebrities were always hanging out in old Vegas. Even, from time to time, on the golf course…

Once in a while I played golf at the Sahara Country Club. It was a great course (still is by the way) and very inexpensive to play. One afternoon, it was a weekday as I recall, I was playing by myself. I snap hooked a drive to the left and it went into someone's back yard.

There was a low fence between the fairway and the yard. The ball didn't go in very far, so I thought it might be possible to reach over and grab my ball. I looked over the fence and I saw a man sitting by his pool.

It was Johnny Carson.

Johnny was relaxing by the pool listening to music and reading the newspaper. Never one to be shy, I spoke right up and shouted, "Sir?"

Johnny put his paper down, looked over at me and said, "Yea?"

"My ball came in your yard. I was wondering if I could hop over the fence and come get it." I could see my ball clearly now about five feet from the fence.

"Sure," Johnny said. "It'll only cost ya ten dollars."

"What?" I said.

"Ten dollars," Johnny repeated. "That's the price for your ball."

"Well… ah…," I stammered. "Just forget it."

Johnny started laughing and said, "I'm just bustin' your chops. Come in and get it."

There was a gate in the fence near to where I was standing. I opened the gate, walked in the yard and retrieved my ball. Johnny got up and stood by me.

"Mr. Carson," I said, "thanks so much." We shook hands. We shot the breeze for a minute. I went back to my golf game, Johnny went back to his newspaper.

I told the guys back in the clubhouse the story. They told me that was Johnny's house in Vegas, he stayed there when he was working or just visiting town.

Louis Prima was one of the nicest people in the world. Louis was a jazz band leader, he played the trumpet and he sang. He was a Vegas icon. Louis played almost every night in the lounge at the Sahara. That's where we met and became friends. We found that we shared a common passion, golf.

I was playing golf with Louis one day and I said to him, "I'd love to have copies of some of your music."

"Come over to the house and pick up the albums," Louis said. "You got a tape recorder?"

"I do," I told him.

"Just give me a call," Louis said, "and come on over and pick up the albums, Jimmy."

A month later or so I was ready to make copies of Louis' albums. I called him up and asked if it would be okay if I came over.

"Maybe later, Jim. I'm not feeling so good right now," Louis said.

"Oh sure, Louis," I said. "Get well soon."

Louis didn't get well, he died later that year, 1978, in New Orleans. That was Louis' hometown. Many, many nights I sat and watched Louis and his orchestra perform. He was a phenomenal musician. A lot of people remember him from the 1967 Disney movie *Jungle Book*. The character King Louis was voiced by Louis Prima. He had a ton of hits in the 50s and 60s like *The Wildest, Jump, Jive an' Wail and Just a Gigolo*.

Anyone who lived in Vegas in the 60s and 70s could tell you about Louis Prima. He was truly one of the greats.

# The Duke and Elvis

After a while, I left the Mint and went to work at the Hilton. It was better than the Mint, definitely a step up. When I got on the stick at a craps game at the Hilton, I'd do impersonations. I do John Wayne and say, "Well, there comin' out. Get yer bets down." Or Walter Brennan, "Hey, comin' out, getyer, getyer, getyer bets down. How much ya wan' on the hard four?" Jimmy Stewart was always a favorite, "Well, ah, here we go. Bet the money now." I loved my Jimmy Cagney bit, "How much you want you dirty rat on the hard ten."

People loved my antics and it became kinda my signature. It livened everybody up, made people laugh and in no way diminished my professionalism or control of the game. The bosses, they loved it too. The happier people are, the more likely they are to bet and stay around longer.

One night Elvis was appearing at the Hilton. Big crowd, but there were no customers at the time because the show was going on. We were standing around shooting the breeze, waiting to go to work. As soon as the show was over, people walked out on to the casino floor looking to gamble.

One of the first people to emerge from the showroom that night was John Wayne. That's right, the legendary actor himself. This was a few years before his death, so he was still in good health and looked just like he did in the movies. He was wearing a nice pair of slacks, cowboy boots, fringed brown jacket and a Western style hat. It looked like he was ready to go on set and start filming.

He walked straight over to my table. He stood right next to me. Mr. Wayne reached into his pocket and grabbed five one hundred dollar bills.

"Can I have some change please," Mr. Wayne said to me.

I put the bills in front of the box man and then I reached out and cut $500 in checks. The game started.

My boss came over to me whispered in my ear and said, "Okay, Jim. Let's hear you do John Wayne now."

I stood there for a few minutes, doing my job and I thought about it. I said to myself silently, "You know what? I may never get this chance again."

I was six foot four and 230 pounds at the time and in decent shape. Mr. Wayne was taller than me and had to outweigh me by twenty pounds. I looked at Mr. Wayne and said in my best John Wayne voice, "Well howya doin' Mr. Wayne?"

Mr. Wayne laughed, reached over and slapped me on the shoulder and said, "That's a helluva lot better than some of these assholes are doin' me." Mr. Wayne kept laughing.

My boss roared, as did everyone else at the table.

Mr. Wayne stayed for another twenty minutes until he lost his five bills. He threw some dough in for the dealers, shook my hand and went on his

way. It was one of the greatest moments of my life. Me, Jim nobody from Canton, spending a little time with the Duke himself.

That was Vegas back in the day. You just never knew who you might run into.

Elvis' run at the Hilton was ending right about this same time. I told my girlfriend, Liz, that we should probably go see Elvis before his run was over. You never know if Elvis will be back or when, etc. So I got tickets for the Sunday night show.

The Friday before we were set to go to the show I was taking a break in the Employees Dining Room, the EDR. The food was great in the EDR but that night I wasn't eating on my break, I was watching a ball game on TV in a side room. So I'm sitting there watching the tube and who comes walking into the room…

Elvis Presley.

Elvis walked up to me and asked, "How ya doin?"

I said, "Great! Just on break watching the game on TV."

Elvis asked me, "What's your name?"

"Jim Sinay."

We laughed and shook hands. Elvis said, "Whaddya do here?"

"I'm a craps dealer on a break."

"Where ya from originally?" Elvis asked me.

"Canton Ohio," I said, still not quite believing that I was shooting the breeze with Elvis Presley.

"I've never been to Canton," Elvis said. "I've heard all about Ohio football and sports in general."

"Yea," I said. "If you were raised back there you played some kind of sport."

"Have you seen my show yet?" Elvis asked.

"No, but I'm bringing my girl to see you this Sunday night."

"What's your girl's name?" Elvis asked.

"Liz," I answered.

"Jim, I'll tell ya what. You bring her close to the stage and I'll sing a song to her."

"You're kidding," I said.

"No," Elvis said. "I'll do it. We work in the same place, you seem like a nice guy, I'll do it for ya."

"Bless your heart," I said.

Elvis was with a hotel security guy, his personal bodyguard Red West and another guy I did not recognize. "Gotta go, Jimmy. See ya Sunday night," Elvis said and left.

I'd met a couple of entertainers before and they were okay people, but I thought well, Elvis Presley? Would he really do that for me? I didn't say

much to anybody and I didn't say anything to Liz. If I did tell her about it and Elvis didn't sing a song to her she would feel really bad.

Sunday night rolled around. The Maître D knew me pretty well because we both worked together, so he sat us in the fifth row from the stage. Elvis did his show – some girls came up to the stage and he gave them a scarf, then he went back for another scarf, gave it to another girl, kissed them on the cheek, etc. Typical Elvis.

Eventually, Elvis looked over my way. I put my arm around Liz and lifted my finger up behind her and pointed down. Elvis nodded his head! I was stunned. I said in my mind, "Oh my God! He's really gonna do it!"

Elvis turned his back to us, facing the other side of the theatre and he said, "Ladies and Gentlemen, a friend of mine is in the audience tonight. He brought his girl in to see the show. This next song I'm gonna do is dedicated to my friend."

Elvis then turned and faced us and pointed right at Liz and me. "Liz honey, this is for my friend Jimmy, from me to you." And then Elvis starts signing, "I want you, I need you, I love you."

Liz could not breathe. She was completely overwhelmed. The people all around me tapped me on the shoulder and said, "You know Elvis?" I had to puff a bit.

"Yea," I said, playing it up for all it was worth. "I work here at the Hilton. I know him."

What a night that was. Liz thanked me for that for years to come. Always wondered what happened to Liz. Like so many friends from my past, we've simply lost touch.

# The Binions and the Italian Club

Back in 1946 when Bugsy Seigel was building the Flamingo Hotel on what would become the Las Vegas Strip, Benny Binion moved to Sin City from Dallas, Texas and opened a gambling hall on Fremont Street that he called Binion's Horseshoe Club. You can do a little research on Benny and see what others have to say about him. There is no doubt that Benny was one tough son of a bitch. He had a well-deserved reputation for being a guy you did not cross, but was also well known for being a fair and honest gambling man.

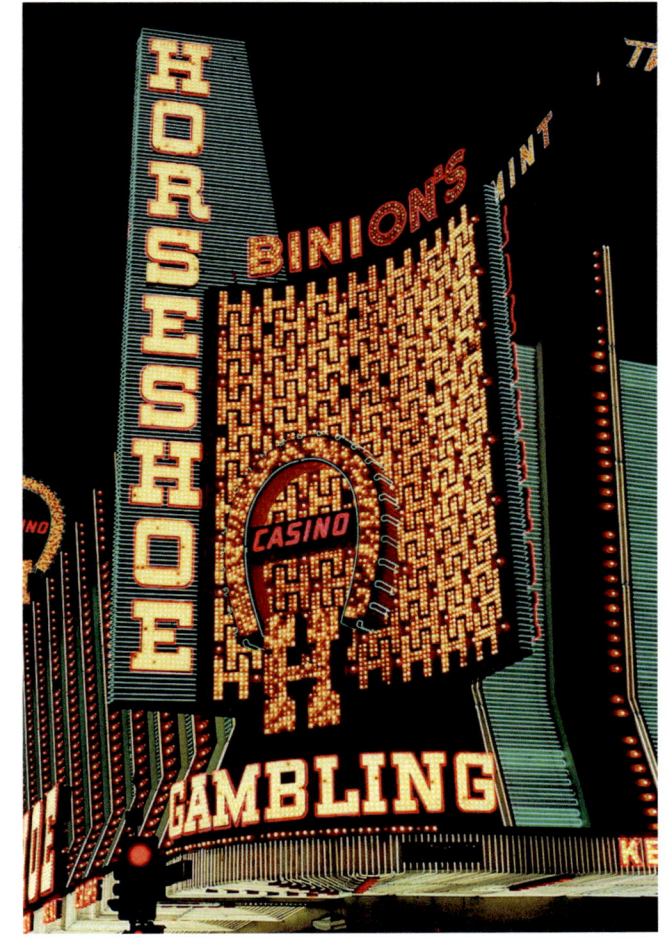

Benny didn't like the idea of building a hotel on his property (although his kids eventually did that) and he wasn't much for providing entertainment or fancy restaurants to his patrons. His oft quoted famous line about such things was, "I don't want to see my money blown out of the end of some guy's trumpet." What Benny did, better than anyone else, was give anyone who wanted to gamble in his joint a fair deal. He was famous for covering any bet anyone wanted to make in his casino. If you had a million bucks in a bag and you wanted to put it on the pass line and roll the dice, Benny would "fade" (cover) you no questions asked.

Trouble was, Benny's Dallas past caught up with him in the mid-1950s and he got nailed on a tax evasion beef in 1953. He did 42 months in prison. After that, Benny could not go on the casino floor. His children had to "officially" run his gambling hall because he lost his gaming license. I knew three of Benny's kids fairly well – Jack, Teddy and Barbara.

My roomie in the early 70s was a guy named Rick Benedict. Rick was pals with Barbara Binion. From the very first time Rick introduced me to Barb, I knew that I'd met somebody special. She was good people, as nice as they come. Barb treated me like an old friend from the moment we said hello.

In fact, my very first Christmas in Vegas would have been very lonely if it were not for the Binion family. Barb and Teddy invited me over to their house for food, drink and good company. Remember, I was Jimmy Nobody, a kid from Ohio. These were some of the most famous people in Vegas, legends in fact.

**Jimmy And His Brother Bob At The Horseshoe**

Benny made a point of thanking me for keeping an eye on Barb and Rick because, well, those two liked to drink. And by like to drink, I mean they liked to drink. Well past the point of excess. When this happened I'd pick them up and drop them off if I wasn't working. There is no use in sugar coating it – the Binion family had its share of substance abuse problems. Doesn't mean they weren't good people, or that they weren't good to me.

Teddy loved to party and he loved the pretty girls. If Teddy was your friend, then he was your friend. He was extremely loyal to people, often to a fault. In the years I knew him best, the 1970s, Teddy would walk around the Horseshoe and "take care of things" as they came up. If you got caught cheating or stealing in the Horseshoe you had to answer to Teddy and, believe me, that's not something you wanted to do.

Once in a while I got asked to hang out with Teddy or do this and that with him. I politely passed almost every time. Why? Teddy was into things that were not good for his health, most notably heroin, and I wanted no part of that. What I'm saying here is not news to anyone who read the Vegas newspapers in the 1990s, but Teddy flat out made some bad choices in life. That said, he was a good guy with some bad habits. I've known plenty of people who were rotten, bad habits or not, and I want to tell you that the Binions were real nice folks.

Jack ran the casino back in the day. He was a hard working person and while he was definitely in charge of the joint, Benny was always nearby. Benny was allowed to sit in the coffee shop or at the bar, both of which were close to the action. I never worked in the Horseshoe, but I was in there a lot, especially in the early 1970s.

It was in the Shoe where I learned my lesson about gambling the hard way. Like a lot of people, when I was young I thought that maybe I could make some money gambling. So after work, I went to the Horseshoe and played craps and 21. Back then I didn't have much dough, so when I lost I really felt the pain. I didn't take long for me to understand why the Binions were rich and I wasn't – the only way to get rich in the gambling business was to be the house.

But I saw and heard a few things playing dice and cards in the old Shoe…

One night Benny was sitting at the bar. There was a craps game going on not fifty feet away from him. Someone Benny knew well, a friend of his I'm sure, was sitting right next to him and betting big money. This guy was dropping or winning ten grand plus on every roll. After every roll, the stickman was calling out the dice… no, he was shouting out the dice. I mean you could hear this guy yell, "Winner, front line seven" or "Six, point is six" all the way to Mexico.

But the stickman wasn't yelling loud enough. "Call them dice out loud!" Benny shouted from his seat at the bar.

What Benny was doing was keeping track of the bettor's action on the bar with Lammers. Every time the shooter won or lost 10K he'd put down a Lammer. After half an hour of this, Benny's friend was through betting. The guy was in the hole 20 grand, but both he and Benny were smiling and drinking.

One of my best memories of Barb Binion was when she was over at our apartment at the Patrician Arms one night. I wanted to make some marinara sauce or "gravy" as the Italians call it. We were feeding a large number of people that night. I didn't have a pot nearly big enough to do the job.

"What size pot do you need, Jimmy?" Barb asked me.

"Maybe one twice this size or larger," I said, holding up a pot that was 12 inches wide 12 inches deep.

"Drive me over to the Horseshoe?" Barb asked.

"Why are we going to the Shoe?" I asked.

"You wanna big pot, right?" she said.

So we jumped in my caddy and drove to the Horseshoe. Barb walked us through the place and back to the main kitchen. Looking at the wall, I saw a number of large cooking pots hanging there.

"Pick one, Jim. Which one do you need?" Barb asked me.

I looked around and saw the right one. It was huge. "The third pot from the right will do."

Barb told the cook to take it down. He handed me the pot and we left. That night I cooked sauce for a ton of people. To this very day, I still have that pot.

It's stories like this, small acts of kindness shown to so many people, that illustrate why we loved the Binions. If there was ever any family that epitomized old Vegas it was them – for better and for worse.

Barb died of an overdose in the early 80s. In the next decade Teddy followed her the same way, although his overdose wasn't accidental. Their deaths made me sad. They were too nice of people to go out that way. The old Horseshoe Club fell apart at the end of the 1990s – court battles, deaths, drama, it was an ugly mess.

But When It Was Great, the Horseshoe was the best downtown Vegas had to offer. Personally, I think Benny is turning over in his grave when he looks at Fremont Street nowadays. The street is closed to cars and it's covered, kinda like a living museum to what it once was. All the old joints now are nothing more than tourist traps. That's not what Benny had in mind back in 1946. What Benny built was a place where anyone who wanted to place a fair bet could do it 24/7 and get fair odds. After some gambling, if you wanted some good American food, a steak and potato, you could get that at the Shoe too for less than three bucks.

Oh, and by the way, next time you're in Vegas and you're enjoying that complimentary drink the casino is serving you while you gamble say thanks to Benny Binion. Giving away booze to gamblers was his idea and it was first done in the Horseshoe Club.

♠♦♣♥     ♥♣♦♠

As you might gather from the name, the old Italian Club in Vegas catered to a certain clientele. Now, not every Italian in Vegas was a made guy, not hardly. But higher profile social events frequented by men who looked like they stepped off the set of *The Sopranos*? Well, let's just say you didn't need a program to follow the play.

Every month a group of guys went to this bar/restaurant and shared a great meal. We shot the breeze about this or that and had a good time. I really looked forward to these events. I wanted to stay in good graces with the fellas. If I needed something, a favor, help getting out of a jam, anything, these were the guys I turned to. Also, you never wanted to get on their bad side or have them think you weren't sociable.

I usually went to these dinners with my good buddy Tony. The food was always top notch. The wine, however…

Late one afternoon we were at the club and Al (name changed to protect the guilty) came over to the table, bottle of red wine in hand.

"Jimmy, Tony. I wanted to share something special with you today. This wine has been aged for a couple of decades. If you could buy it, which you can't, it'd cost ya over $400 a bottle. I'd like to pour you fellas a glass."

"Hey Al," I said. "Thanks. I'd love to sample your wine."

Al poured Tony and me a small glass and then moved on to another guest and made him the same offer. I picked up my glass, clinked it with

Tony's glass and we took a sip. We both looked at each other and we could read each other's minds – the wine was horrible! I don't mean bad, I mean undrinkable.

I looked at Tony and he looked at me. We eyeballed Al and, thank God, he was busy serving other guests. There was just no way Tony and I could hide our facial expressions when we first tasted the wine.

"Oh my God," I whispered to Tony. "That wine is really nasty."

"I know. Wait, here comes Al," Tony said.

Al walked back over to our table with a huge smile on his face. "How'd you like the wine?" he asked.

"Outstanding," I lied. "Incredible, Al. Just incredible."

"Really good," Tony said, as he held up his glass.

"Only the best for my friends," Al said as he poured a little more into Tony's glass.

As the lethal wine bottle was making its way towards my glass I said, "Thanks, Al but I have to pass. I've had a lot to drink already and I don't want to get a DUI. I apologize."

"Of course, Jimmy. We don't need any trouble with the law," Al said as he winked at me. Then Al walked off looking for other victims.

"Drink up, partner," I said to Tony.

"Don't say a word, Jimmy. You know how sensitive some of the boys are," Tony whispered.

"Let's just sip it slowly. Think of it as bad tasting medicine," I said.

So that's what we did. We sipped the wine slowly and poured the remnants out into another wine glass when Al wasn't looking. You flat out never disrespected these guys. That would be a very stupid thing to

do. They were so good to us working stiffs anyway, from our point of view they had earned our respect.

I played gin once in a while with these old Italian guys. Most of them were in their 60s and 70s. They had some great names like Big Foot Denny and Sleepy Sal. Gianni Russo, the actor from *The Godfather*, often stopped by and chit chatted. He told me a story about the scene where James Caan's character comes after his character for beating up Caan's character's sister. Caan came after Russo with the top of a garbage can. I guess it wasn't all play acting. Gianni said Caan hit him twice really hard. Gianni tried to tell him to ease off, but Caan was totally into the part. After the scene was over, Gianni showed Jimmy Caan the scrapes and bruises on his arms. James Caan apologized profusely.

The women adored Gianni Russo. He was a handsome fella and a really nice man. He owned a small bar on State Street. He tried to build his own gambling joint, but for one reason or another it never got off the ground.

Anyway… In those gin games, after two or three discards they knew exactly what you had in your hand. They were tough to beat. We played for $5 a game and so much per point. It wasn't about the money, it was about the pride. The few times I was able to win a game or two from them I left there feeling like I'd conquered Rome.

# Femme Fatales

I love women. I respect them too. I've always believed that women deserve to be paid as much as men and to be treated equally with men in the workplace. I like to think of myself as a good time guy, but also as a man who would never hit or verbally abuse a gal. Maybe I wasn't good husband material, but I always tried to be a good friend.

Having said all that, some women in Vegas back in the day… To be fair some men too… Let's just say it got really interesting at times…

Don, my roommate, tended bar at the Chateau Vegas. He went to work at eight at night and got off around four in the morning. One night I was out at The Flame drinkin' with my buddies. We were having a good time. By the time I got home it was late, or rather it was very early in the morning. I decided not to go to bed, but to walk over to the Chateau. Don was still working, his shift wasn't over yet.

I noticed what I thought was a very attractive girl sitting at the bar. Don gave me a drink and I told him, "Give her one too."

Don looked at me kinda strange and said, "Give her a drink?" He motioned with his head to make sure we were talking about the same lady.

"Yea," I said. It had been a fun but a long night. Who knows? I said to myself, maybe I'll get lucky and have someone to keep my feet warm tonight.

When she got her drink the lady said to me, "Thanks, honey."

"Would you like some company?" I asked.

"Sure," she said, so I moved over a stool closer to her and we started talking. Now I'd not only had a few that night, but a few too many. She told me where she lived. We got cozy real fast.

"I gotta roommate," I said, pointing at Don. "Can't go to my place, wanna go to yours?"

"Yea, let's go," she said.

I paid my tab and followed her out. As I was leaving, Don was smiling at me in an odd sorta way. I wondered what the hell he was smiling about, what was so damn funny. Pinky, as always, was parking cars. The lady had already paid Pinky and he was getting her car.

Standing there under the streetlight this lady turned and looked at me. She was, without a doubt, one of the ugliest broads I'd ever seen in my life. I mean this woman, God bless her, she got hit with every branch of the ugly tree when she tumbled out of the treehouse. I almost went home with a gargoyle.

When her car arrived she said, "You know where I live."

"I'll be right there," I said.

When she drove off, I went back inside the Chateau. Don was there to greet me, he was just getting off his shift. He yelled out, "I told you guys when he saw her in the light he'd be back! You two," Don says pointing at a couple of guys at the bar, "owe me five bucks each!"

"No more drinkin' for you pal!" Don said to me. "You almost made a really bad mistake!"

What could I say? Sometimes I went too far. Thank goodness for friends to keep me in line.

Women. It was always somethin'…

For a while, I dated two ladies at the same time. To make it even more complicated and confusing, they were both named Patty. I had asked Patty number one out to dinner one night to Bob Taylor's Ranch House, an old favorite of mine. I was getting dressed and ready to go when the phone rang. Don, my roomie, answered the phone. I heard him talking to someone and then he hung up.

"Jim?" Don yelled at me.

"Yea?" I said.

"That was Pat. She said that she'd meet you over at The Flame."

"Okay," I said. No problem, I could meet her there before we went out to eat.

I went to The Flame and walked inside. There sitting at the bar was Patty. Only it wasn't the Patty I had a date with, it was Patty number two. I didn't want to lose Patty number two, so we started talking.

"Sorry I called you, Jimmy," Patty number two said, "I just wanted to talk with you for a bit."

So we talked and had a drink. I kept thinking in my mind, what kind of excuse can I give her to leave? I didn't want to make her angry and she just kept on talking and talking. One thing led to another and Patty number two and I went to a couple of different places. My brain, granted my brain doesn't always work the best where women are concerned, suggested to me that I could call Patty number one later and tell her that I got called to work on an emergency, etc. – make up some excuse.

Patty number two and I got back to my place around ten or so. We were sitting in the living room, listening to music and having a cocktail when there was a knock on the door. I went to the door and answered it. It was Patty number one.

I said, oh my God. What am I gonna do?

So I let Pat in the house. I introduced the two ladies. I poured Pat number one a glass of wine. Both of these lovely ladies were cocktail waitresses at different hotel casinos. For a moment or two no one said a word.

Standing in the middle of the room I said this, "Girls, it doesn't matter what I say or do. I'm dead meat right now. There's no gettin' out of what's goin' on here. So I'm gonna go upstairs, lay down and turn on the TV."

I went upstairs, turned on the TV, put the pillow behind my back and watched a show. Five minutes later I heard the door close. Five minutes

after that I heard the door slam. I went down and locked the door. I went to bed.

The next day when I woke up I said, "I gotta make this right." So I called up Patty number two.

"I need to see you and explain somethin' to ya," I said. She didn't want to see me again at first, but then she agreed. So we met.

"That other Patty that you met, she came and knocked on my door. She's been trying to go out with me for a long time. I've tried to tell her I'm not the guy for her, but she just wouldn't listen."

Well, Patty number two went for it. She left, had to go to work. So I called the other Patty up.

I explained to Patty number one that Patty number two was my ex-girlfriend and that she came around once in a while and wanted to talk about getting back together. Patty number one seemed satisfied with this explanation.

I kept on dating both of them, but I never got my signals crossed again. Also, I vowed not to date two girls with the same name.

My buddy, Donnie, met this girl, Alice. They had a few drinks, one thing led to another and she asked him over to her place. Alice lived in a second floor apartment in North Las Vegas. There was an outside staircase and balcony that led up to her front door. They talked for a while then they jumped into bed and went at it. After a bit, Donnie got up and walked into the kitchen – he was thirsty and wanted a drink.

Donnie was standing there drinking a glass of water when he heard footsteps coming up the stairway.

"Hey," Donnie said, "you gotta roommate?"

"No, why?" Alice asked.

"Someone is coming up the stairs," Donnie explained.

Alice leapt out of bed and ran to the front door. She peeked out the spy hole and said, "My God! It's my husband!"

"What!" Donnie said. "You didn't say you were married!"

"Well, we're gettin' a divorce but he still lives here and we're still married."

"I'm gone," Donnie said. "Where's the back door?"

"I don't have one," Alice said.

So Donnie, realizing the potential trouble he was in, grabbed his clothes and his shoes and headed for the bathroom. He was stark naked. He opened the bathroom window and looked out. Eight feet below him was the roof of a parking garage. Realizing he didn't really have a choice, it was four a.m. and pitch black outside, he jumped.

Donnie made it to the ground in one piece – he slid down the roof on his bare butt and landed on the cement. He got up, picked up his clothes and started to walk away.

Then Donnie heard, "You son of a bitch!" The husband was yelling at him from the open bathroom window he'd just left. Donnie picked up the pace and that was a good thing because seconds later two bullets went whizzing by him.

Donnie went into a full sprint down the alley. He turned left, then right and then made his way out to an open area with a tree. He was naked as a jaybird, holding his clothes, leaning against this tree completely out of breath.

After a few seconds, Donnie started to put on his clothes. He couldn't see anyone around, but he had this strange feeling that somebody was watching him. After he had got his pants and shirt on and he was fumbling

with his shoes, Donnie looked across the alley and saw an elderly black couple. They were sitting on a bench and watching Donnie get dressed.

The old guy was drinking something from a paper bag and smiling, but his wife was shaking her head and waging her finger at him saying without words, "You naughty boy. What have you been doing?"

Donnie didn't say a word, but he stayed out of sight and made his way back to his car which was thankfully not parked in front of Alice's place. He started his car and pulled away as fast as he could without turning on his headlights.

My friend learned a valuable lesson – in Vegas, never assume that someone's married or unmarried. You better get to know them a little bit before you make that judgment.

When it came to women and using good judgment, well, Donnie had some bad luck …

Donnie met a girl who lived on the ground floor of an apartment building. He took her home one night, back to her place. Things went well, so Donnie called her up the next day and asked if she would like to see him again. She said yes and Donnie told her he'd be over after work around two a.m. in the morning.

One problem. When Donnie got back to her place around two, he looked at the row of doors on the ground floor. They all looked the same. Damned if he could remember which place was hers. He couldn't recall her apartment number.

Then he got some inspiration. He was pretty sure that she lived in apartment six, the sixth one from the end. He looked at the door and more information hit his brain, he remembered that she said she had a

pink flower on her door. Sure enough, there was a pink flower on door number six. So he knocked a couple of times. No answer.

Now Donnie had downed a few martinis by this point so he had some liquid courage motivating him. He decided to go in the back of this girl's place and climb in through the bedroom window. Maybe she was asleep or in the shower. He'd surprise her.

When he got 'round back, he started counting the windows. Trouble was, he couldn't be sure if he had the right place or not. He thought he did, he had confidence. The window was only about five feet off the ground. He reached up and slid the window open.

Ol' Donnie started to crawl in and the lights came on. He was looking straight at something now, but it wasn't his gal. It was the barrel of 357 Magnum pointed right at his head.

There were a man and wife in this apartment, both of them in their 50s. They thought Donnie was trying to rob 'em.

"Don't move," the man said. "You're in deep trouble man."

"I'm in the wrong place. I'm looking for my girlfriend."

"Who's your girlfriend?"

Donnie told the man his girl's name.

"She's next door, dumbass!" the man yelled. "We got robbed a week ago. I keep this Clint Eastwood cannon next to my bed now. You're lucky your head is still attached to your neck. Get out of here and don't bother us again."

"I'm so sorry," Donnie said as he backed out of the window. Then he went to the right window and talked with his girl who let him in.

That sounds funny, and it was in hindsight. But people got killed doing stupid things back in the day.

I knew someone, he was a nice guy, a card dealer. He was about my age. It wouldn't be right to use his name – you'll soon understand why. My friend fell in love with a gal who had a daughter who was nine or ten. They were all set to get married and they were living together.

My friend came home one night after work and hopped in the shower. When he was done he forgot to get a towel, so he had to get one from the hall closet. So, buck naked, he walks in the hallway. Who's there? The little girl. She only had panties on. She had been sleeping, woke up and was looking for something. Embarrassing for sure, but it quickly became much more.

At that moment, the girl's mother came home. There was her fiancé standing naked with her little girl. She thought the worst, the guy was

fooling around with her daughter. The little girl was too scared to say anything when mom pulled out her pistol from her purse.

She shot my friend three times despite his protests that nothing bad was going on. Later, when she was calm, the little girl told the police exactly what happened. Needless to say, the woman's mother was held accountable by the authorities for manslaughter.

Getting done in by a woman. That was Vegas. Yea, it happened to me too, although in a slightly different way…

I was home recovering from hemorrhoid surgery. A gal I'd been dating for a few months, Eileen, was tending to me. I really liked Eileen and while I wasn't ready for the altar, I was thinking about living with her. She seemed to have all the qualities I was looking for in a long term relationship, numbers one and two on that list being genuine feelings for me and integrity.

Now, if you've ever had to suffer through hemorrhoid surgery then you know how painful that is. For the first couple of days after I left the hospital I was hurtin' real bad. I had pain meds and between that and some scotch I just laid on the couch and prayed that the time would pass as quickly as possible.

I wasn't exactly at my best. Eileen was in the kitchen. She was a great cook. She popped out of the kitchen and came over to the couch, a piece of paper in hand.

"Honey, would you sign this for me?" Eileen said.

"Let me look at it," I said. I read the paper and I couldn't figure out what the hell it was. I couldn't read too well with all the meds and it was written in legalese. But my internal radar was going off, I knew that something was up.

I grabbed the phone and called my buddy Billy. Despite my foggy brain, somehow I managed to dial his number.

"Bill," I said. "Eileen wants me to sign something. I don't know what the hell it is. I'm down for the count over here."

"I'll be right over," Billy said.

Maybe half an hour later Billy showed up. "What's she want ya to sign?" he asked me. I handed Bill the paper. He read it.

"Jimmy, this paper says that you are giving Eileen half the house you're going to buy and half the money you're going to make at the casino in exchange for her living with you for one year."

"You're kidding," I said. I was floored, but I was also completely out of it.

"You want me to handle it?" Billy asked.

"Yea, please," I said.

Billy went into the kitchen, pointed at the letter and said to Eileen, "You got five minutes to collect your shit and get the hell outta here."

Now Billy was a former Navy Seal. He was a big tough guy. Billy followed her up the stairs and watched her as she put her stuff in a couple of bags. I'm watching all this from my perch on the couch, following most of it, but groggy as hell.

When they went to the front door, she stood there looking at me. Billy said, "You're two seconds late," and he kicked her square in the ass. He knocked her outside the door. "Don't ever come back here again or you'll deal with me. I won't be so nice next time."

**Billy The Navy Seal**

Billy checked on me and said, "I'll be back in an hour or so. I'll make sure you got what you need, Jimmy."

After Billy left I sat there thinking, "Why me? What did I do to deserve to be treated like that?"

Years later we heard that Eileen left town and moved to California. She married a banker. Poor bastard. If she was the type to take advantage of someone like me in my condition, she was capable of almost anything.

# The Sahara

The time had come for me to move up in the dealing world. I got an audition at the Sahara Hotel. In the 70s, the Sahara was one of the top joints on the strip. At the Sahara, I was making $25 a day in salary and the tokes were up to $100 to $150 a day. I worked there for several years.

While I could deal more than one game, my favorite was craps. Craps is a fun, exciting game. There is a lot of action – and by that I mean there is always something for the dealer to do; pay off a bet, put on a bet, take another bet off, etc. etc.

Sometimes at a craps table the dice are what we call "spitting". By spitting I mean that a shooter will make a point and then roll a bunch of other numbers and then roll his point number before he rolls seven. Winner after winner. This is when players can clean up in a hurry by betting on the numbers. A good shooter can keep shooting for 25 to 30 minutes.

One night we had a great game going. I had about seven or eight players on my end of the table. The bets were flowin', everything was good. Then the dice came to a little old lady. Think about an iconic picture of a grandmother – small, grey hair, glasses and an old fashioned dress. That was her. She was standing next to the stickman on my end of the table.

At a craps game, the shooter is supposed to throw the dice so they hit the far wall and bounce back on the table. This ol' gal had a hard time throwin' the dice that far, but she had no trouble rolling her number.

If the old lady made a point of eight, she'd roll an eight, usually after rolling three or four numbers in between. She threw plenty of sevens, but only on the come out roll. People were lovin' this lady! More folks crowded around. Not once did the dice hit the far wall.

The Floor Supervisor, he's standing there watching the whole thing. He doesn't say a word until the lady has "passed", rolled her number before she rolls seven, seven times. On the come out roll she threw a winner seven. Then she made a point of ten. Money is stackin' up on the pass line – everyone is betting with her. Then she rolls two fives, a hard way ten.

The table erupts. Now people are standing two and three deep watching the action and/or desperately trying to get close enough to bet.

So the Floor Supervisor says to the stickman, "Tell the lady to roll the dice to the end of the table and hit the wall."

The Stick says to the old lady, "Ma'am, please roll the dice so they hit the wall down there at the end."

The old lady nodded her head. She threw the dice again. One of them hit the wall, the other one did not. She made a point of five. Everybody piled on the bets. This lady had made her number seven straight times. She rolled the dice again – both short of the wall. Winner five! The dealers paid off the bets, people were screaming and hollering. We're all making money – the tips were great and the customers were making bets for the dealers.

The Floor Supervisor again put himself between me and the stickman and said, "Tell the lady to throw the dice to the end of the table and hit the wall."

"Ma'am, please throw the dice and hit the wall," the stickman told her.

She nodded her head and said okay. She made another number, a nine. On the third roll she rolled another winner, nine. I'm paying off the bets. People were going insane.

The Floor Supervisor stuck his head between me and the stickman and yelled, "Tell this fuckin' broad to roll those fuckin' dice to the end of the fuckin' table!"

The stickman looked at the old lady and then back at the Floor Supervisor. Then he said as he pointed at the Floor Supervisor, "Ma'am that man right there," the Stick said, "wants me to tell you to throw the fuckin' dice to the end of the fuckin' table and hit the fuckin' wall." The

Stick was laughing so hard he could barely get the words out of his mouth. The Floor Supervisor disappeared.

Everybody roared. The old lady rolled five more numbers before she sevened out. We all made money.

I don't know what the world's record is for consecutive passes at a craps table. Me, I've seen someone do it twenty times – roll twenty numbers before rolling seven. But in my decades dealing craps that is very rare. If you're ever lucky enough to run into that kinda streak, I hope you have plenty of money to bet.

I had some great friends at the Sahara. We'd hang out after work, go out for drinks and have a few laughs. One night when we were out I met this girl. She was gorgeous and really nice. I took her home to my place. When we got to my apartment, we went directly to the bedroom. She took a minute and used the bathroom.

I'd made a "score" that night. A score for a dealer was a shift where you made a lot of tokes. I'd made $1500, which was huge money for me back in the day. Obviously, between the girl and the dough and the drinks, I was on cloud nine. I said to myself, I gotta hide this cash! So I did, or at least I thought I did.

The girl came back, we went to bed and nature took its course. She spent the night. The next morning she got up around nine or ten, gave me a kiss and said, "Thanks, Jimmy."

"Thanks, baby doll," I said. I was still in bed. My head was throbbing from a major hangover. The girl left and I lay there for a while, recovering.

When I made a couple of hundred bucks or more in tokes, I used to hide the money in my suit coat pockets or in my boots. So when I got out of bed I went to the closet and looked for my $1500. I checked all

my usual hiding places. There was no money. I tried as hard as I could to recall exactly where I stashed the dough, but I was out of it at the time. I just couldn't remember.

I went through every inch of my room. I checked the dresser, under the mattress and in the closet again. My money was gone.

"Damn it!" I said. "That girl ripped me off for $1500!"

I didn't have this girl's phone number, her address, anything. I couldn't even remember her name! For about a week I tried to find out who she was, where she lived, but I could not track her down. I knew she worked somewhere on the Strip as a cocktail waitress, but damn if I could remember where it was.

After a couple of weeks, I just gave up. I chalked it up to experience. Things like that just happened in Vegas, what the heck was I gonna do.

One day my roomie and I decided it was time to clean up our place. We didn't live in filth, but we weren't the neatest guys on the planet. When the dirt piled up too high, we broke out the brooms and the cleaning solutions and went at it.

I was cleaning the lamps and the lights. I went into my bedroom and started dusting everything off. I started on the dresser, moved into the bathroom, kept working. There was a light above my bed. I had a shade on it that hung down. I could see that there was dust all over the shade.

When I unscrewed the light shade and took it off, out fell fifteen one hundred dollar bills. What I'd done in my less than sober state was stood on the bed and put the money in the shade.

For the past couple of months I'd been making bad remarks about this lady, even though I didn't know a thing about her. Now, as it turns out, I was to blame for the whole thing. I felt bad about that. A person's

reputation is everything. I take such matters very seriously. I'm so glad that I didn't know who she was because if I had I'd have cussed someone who was totally innocent.

Women and me… Let's just say if I have an Achilles Heel, it's the ladies. I always took to heart and respected what my Uncle Ed told me about Vegas, "Don't lie, cheat or steal, Jimmy. I've got your back if anything else happens to ya."

Uncle Ed didn't say anything to me about getting into trouble with females…

I'd been dealing at the Sahara for a few years. The money was great, I loved the people I worked with and I was having a ball.

I was dating a cocktail waitress. No big deal, I thought. Me dating a cocktail waitress was a pretty routine state of affairs. One day I was standing at a crap game. We were waiting for the show to break. There were no players yet. One of the bosses was about twenty feet away from me. An executive from the hotel was talking to him. I noticed that their conversation was getting a bit animated. The executive was saying something emphatically and pointing at me. The boss was shaking his head "no", but the executive kept barking and pointing at me.

In my mind I said, "What the hell was that all about?" I knew it probably wasn't good, but I also knew that my hands were clean. There was no legitimate reason for an executive to be angry with me.

The show broke and we got some players. A man walked up to the table and made a bet on the pass line. He threw the dice and he lost. Then he made another bet on the pass line and next to it he placed another bet and said, "This is for you."

Dealers made money by players betting for them. This happens every minute of every day in Vegas, then and now. If a dealer asks a player to make a bet for him, that's called hustling. While it's not illegal, hustling is not allowed in casinos. If a player wants to place a bet for you unprompted then fine, but asking for a bet is at best bad form and at worst an offense that can lead to your termination.

At some casinos, the boss will walk away when players are making bets for the dealers. That way dealers and customers can have friendly exchanges which might technically cross the line. Those are the best bosses to have and I had plenty of 'em, especially at the Sahara.

I said to this man who placed a $5 bet for me, "Oh sir, thank you. Why don't you make some money first and then bet for me." I shoved his bet for me off the pass line.

He put the money back on the pass line and said, "Leave it on, it's okay."

I shoved it off again and said, "Give it a little time. You can bet for me later once you've made some dough."

Then the man got testy. He put the bet back on the line and said, "Leave the son of a bitch there."

I do not argue with customers when they are doing something that's allowed even if I don't like what they are doing. That's not my place. So I smiled and left the money alone.

The pit boss came over to the table, saw the bet the man made for me and said, "Um hum," and walked away. I was clueless.

The man lost the bet he made for me and few more bucks and then he went on his way. I didn't think any more of the incident. People bark at dealers for all sorts of reasons – they're pissed that they've lost money, their wife said something nasty to them, their dog won't fetch anymore,

who knows. Pit bosses look at games all the time and nod their heads and move on.

When it was break time, after the stickman tapped me on the shoulder I walked away to take my break. I didn't make it ten feet when the pit boss intercepted me. He handed me a pink slip, a notice of immediate termination.

I said, "What's this for?"

The pit boss said, "What's it say, Jim?"

"Hustling," I said, not believing my eyes. "I didn't do a damn -."

"Jim," the pit boss said, "It ain't from me."

Then I understood. Somebody set me up. It had to be that casino executive. But why in the hell was he angry with me? I truly had no clue.

I walked out of the Sahara and never looked back. My reputation was solid around town. Hustling was by no means a fatal offense even if I was guilty, which I wasn't. I had no trouble getting another job. In fact, I moved up in the world – I became a floor supervisor at the Silverbird Hotel.

A couple of months later while I was working at the Silverbird I was talking with a friend who still worked at the Sahara. He said, "Jim, you know why you got fired from the Sahara, don't you?"

I said, "I have no idea."

He said, "That redhead cocktail waitress you were dating?"

"Yea," I said.

"She was that exec's girlfriend. He's married and you messed up his tidy little arrangement. He found out about your Uncle Ed. He was pissed off because he couldn't break your hands or leg or dump you in a hole in the desert. All he could do was fire ya. That's why he was so hot."

"She told me she was single!" I said.

"That's the way it is Jim," my friend said.

Wow, I said to myself. I would never mess with one of the boys' girlfriends. That was a bad idea. I wasn't in love with this lady, but we saw each other more than once in a while.

I thanked my lucky stars and my Uncle Ed on that one. I could always find another job, but the last thing I needed was one of the boys out to get me because I stole his girl.

# Takin' it a Bit Too Far

There is no denying the fact that I lived through some crazy times. I look back on it now and I just shake my head and say, that's just the way it was. I truly never meant anyone any harm and neither did any of my friends. We just flat out had a good time all the time. There was no other way to live back then as far as we were concerned.

When It Was Great, the Vegas lifestyle was addicting. You just got used to doing your job and then cutting loose. Do I have regrets? Sure. Who doesn't? I also know that I lived through a very unique time in a very unique place.

Now I'm gonna say something that might startle you a bit. Gambling is a sucker's game. What I mean by that is this – if you want to have a good time and you gamble the right way, then it's no big deal. There is only one right way to gamble – take a stack of money you can afford to lose, play the game(s) of your choice, have fun and when you make some dough (whatever you decide in the beginning, double, triple your money etc.) or you lose it all then you stop betting.

Most people can gamble this way, the responsible way. Anyone with a brain should understand the basics of the gambling equation; the house has an edge in every single game. The odds always favor the house. That's why casinos exist because the law of averages never fail over time.

I've seen more'n my share of tragic gambling stories. I'll share a couple with ya…

There was this guy who came in the casino, I won't mention which one, with a suitcase. In this suitcase he had a bunch of cash. The first time I saw him do this he had $150,000 in the suitcase. He asked the casino boss if he could bet all the money in his suitcase at a craps game. His plan was simple enough – put the hundred and fifty grand on the pass line and then roll. Now, as bets go, that's a smart bet. The odds are still with the house, but only barely.

The guy won his bet. The point was made before seven was thrown. So the man went to the casino cage and collected his $300,000.

Sometime later, I think it was a couple of months, this same guy came back with another suitcase. I don't know exactly how much was in it this time, but it was over $300,000. He asked the casino for permission to bet it all on the craps table. Once again, he placed a very smart bet – he put the $300,000 plus on the pass line.

Only this time he lost. Seven came up before the point was made.

The man very calmly thanked us for the game and walked over to the elevator. He got in the elevator and went to the top floor. From the top floor, he took the stairs to the roof. He walked on to the roof and then jumped off. Dropping to the concrete from over twenty stories high will kill you every time.

I watched another guy, a young man in his twenties, play craps all night for big bucks. The casino knew something about him because he had a $150,000 credit line. He went up and down, but by the end of the night he'd lost his entire limit.

He called his father and told him that he owed the casino $150,000. He asked his dad to fly down and cover his gambling debt. The next day the boy's father flew in from somewhere up north, Montana I think it was,

and covered the debt. After he paid the casino the man told his son, "You no longer own half the ranch. Because you were stupid and risked all your money in the casino, you're disinherited."

That young man ended up going to dealer's school and staying in Vegas. Last I heard of him he was doing okay. He became a working stiff like me, which wasn't a bad thing, but to lose a ranch over a night at the tables, that's just plain insanity.

The way to handle gambling is the way you handle any vice – take it in moderation and realize that you're playing with fire. If you have a drinking problem or a drug abuse problem or a gambling addiction, then stay the hell away from Vegas.

I like to drink, but I am not an alcoholic. That said, at times I took booze to an extreme. I remember this one incident at the Go Go Club…

I had a lot of lady friends. I mean the term "lady friend" in the old fashioned sense of that word – these were ladies I dated on and off, but we were not serious about having a relationship. Was I a "player" in the modern sense of that word? No, I wasn't. I was interested in having a good time and I wanted to be with other people who also wanted to have a good time. None of us were into posturing or fancy clothes or conquests or anything like that. All we wanted to do was keep the party going.

It was a fairly routine thing for groups of us to go out partying after our shifts were over. One night five of us were drinking downtown when someone had the idea of going to the Go Go Club on the strip. We'd all had way too much to drink to begin with, but when we got to the Go Go Club we just kept going at it.

It was near dawn when I kinda came out of my stupor. I was sitting in a booth with my lady friend Mary and my other buddies. I looked down at myself and I discovered something that startled me – I was completely naked. I looked over at Mary and she was naked too. My other three friends all had their clothes on.

"What the hell is going on?" I asked my buddy who was sitting next to me.

"Jimmy, you're back!" he said.

"I'm back?" I asked.

"You've been out of it for a while, pal," he said.

At that time, I liked to drink scotch whiskey. After that night I swore off scotch forever…

"Where are my clothes?" I asked.

Just then, I heard Mary laughing. "I bet you $20 that because it was so dark in here no one would notice if we took off our clothes. That was an hour ago. No one's said a word to us."

I looked around and sure enough people were coming and going and girls were dancing on the stage and no one paid us any mind at all. My clothes were piled around my feet. I gathered them up and put them back on. Mary slipped her clothes back on too.

Were we thirty something adults acting like a bunch of teenagers? Yep, that was us alright. We didn't have a care in the world.

My friend Stan told us all that he was finally doing the deed, he was getting married. He'd met this girl in California, they'd dated for a while and she was moving to Vegas. Whenever any of my buddies got married, we went all out and threw them a first class bachelor party.

A first class bachelor party back in the day meant renting a house or a hotel suite, plenty of food and booze and strippers and/or hookers depending on the guy. For Stan's bash, one of my other buddies brought some porno movies. This was in the era before VCRs, so when you showed dirty movies you did it using a projector and a movie screen.

The party was moving right along. The only females present were the strippers. Somebody switched on the porno movie and turned off the lights. I was in the other room talking to a pal when I heard Stan yelling and screaming. He was in distress. From the sound of things, I thought he'd been stabbed or shot.

I went into the room where they were showing the film and all the lights were on and the film had stopped. Stan had his head cradled in his hands and he was crying his eyes out.

"Turn it back on," Stan said through his tears.

"Hey, Stan. Is that such a good idea?" the guy manning the projector asked.

"I gotta know for sure. Switch it back on," Stan said.

So somebody switched the film back on. Stan didn't say a word as he watched a minute or so of this woman having sex with two men on film.

"Shut it off," Stan said. The guy running the projector shut off the film.

"Are you sure?" another guy asked Stan.

"That's her. I can't believe it," Stan said.

As it turns out, Stan's fiancé was the star of the porn film. The poor guy was devastated. He never did get married, to that lady or to anyone else.

I've already told you a little about one of my roommates, Rick Benedict. I loved that guy, what a great person. Ol' Rick, he didn't just drink with Barbara Binion, he could get plenty smashed all on his own…

One morning he walked downstairs in his robe. It looked like last night had been pretty rough.

"How's it going, Rick?" I asked him.

Rick talked in short, brief bursts. "Well… ah…I got drunk last night. Cab driver brought me home. I lost my car."

"You don't know where your car is?" I asked.

"No," Rick answered.

"What happened?" I asked.

"I was off work last night. I started at The Flame. Then I went to the Coachman's, then I went to the Philly. Then I went to another joint on Sahara. I don't remember after that. I went lookin' for my car and it ain't out there."

"What the hell are you gonna do?" I asked.

"I dunno," Rick said.

"Why don't you do this?" I suggested. "You got a motorcycle, right? Start out doing what you did last night. Go to the same places, retrace your path. You'll find your car that way."

Rick said, "That's a good idea."

So Rick hopped on his motorcycle and left. I had to go to work so I didn't see Rick until the next morning. Rick walked down the stairs and sat down across from me.

"Well, did you find your car?" I asked him.

"Nope," Rick said.

"What happened?" I asked.

"I did what you told me to do. I went to The Flame. They told me I went to the Checkerboard. At the Checkerboard, they said I went to the 217. At the 217 they told me I went to the Coachman's. From the Coachman's

they said I went to the Philly Pub. From the Philly Pub, they said I went to the Brewery.

"Now," Rick continued. "Now… I don't where my motorcycle is."

"You lost your motorcycle too?" I asked.

"Yea."

"What the hell are you gonna do?" I asked.

"I dunno," Rick said. "I'll have to tell the police. Somebody stole 'em."

"My God! That's terrible!" Those words had no sooner come out of my mouth when the phone rang. I answered it. There was a girl on the other end.

"Who's this?" the girl asked.

"Jim," I said.

"Rick's your roommate, isn't he?" she asked.

"Yea," I said.

"Well, this is Shirley. Ask your damn roommate to get his car out of my driveway and his motorcycle out of my living room."

"Both Rick's car and his motorcycle are at your place?" I asked.

"For the last two nights we both drank so much that Rick ended up taking a cab home."

"I'll take him over there, Shirley. Hang tight."

So I gathered up Rick and drove him over to Shirley's place. First he retrieved his car and then we went back and he got his motorcycle.

About a week later I was downstairs having breakfast and watching TV. The night before had pretty eventful. I was home the night before, not working. Rick was off too, but he was gone. Around one a.m. I heard a loud knock on my door. It was a cab driver, the same guy who had brought Rick home twice the previous week.

"Ah… I got your roommate downstairs in the cab. Would you mind givin' me a hand with him? The cabbie asked me very politely.

"Sure," I said.

Rick was in the back seat of the cab drunker than a skunk. I helped him out of the cab, propped him up against a wall and went to pay the cabbie.

"Oh no," the cabbie said. "Rick has already paid me. He's a great tipper. Just wanted to be sure he got home safely."

During the minute or two I was talking to the cabbie, Rick had slid down the wall and scraped his face on it. Rick was a large man. There was no way I could carry him up to the apartment. So Rick did all he could do, he crawled up the stairs. The stairs were rough – covered with stucco. It was like he crawled home over sandpaper.

I opened the front door. Then Rick crawled into the apartment and then up the stairs to his bedroom.

Now it was morning and he was standing in front of me again. Rick was scraped up all to hell. His face was scratched where he'd slid down the wall and his knees and arms were also a bloody, scabby mess from crawling up the stucco coated stairs.

Rick looked himself over and said, "That must have been some fight."

"What the hell are you talking about?" I asked him.

"Look at me. Had to be a fight. Wonder what the other guy looks like."

"Rick, there was no fight. You got drunk…" Then I told him the whole story.

"Wow," Rick said.

That cab driver sent Rick a Christmas card every year for the next two years. I always wondered how much money Rick gave that guy.

# Mom Moves to Vegas

My parents got divorced in 1974. Dad was a good man. He made parts for the famous Norton bomb site used by Allied bombers during World War II. After the war, he worked at Ford Motor for 35 years and retired. He was a great bowler and softball player. He was not only a wonderful father to my brother and I, he was also an awesome dad. His boys meant everything to him. Growing up, he always made time for a catch or for me to tell him what was on my mind.

After they divorced, Mom and Dad remained friends for the rest of their lives. More than once they were in Vegas at the same time and we all had dinner together. In 1978, Dad moved to Placerville, California and met a nice lady who he lived with for many years.

Mom moved to Vegas in 1976. She liked to gamble, but she definitely did it the right way. She played low stakes games like Bingo or 25 cent video poker or the dime slots. Then she'd come home and do something else. Mom always called me "Big Dummy" and I always called her "Kid". It was a long standing, corny joke between just us. Mom fell in love with Vegas and it was great having her nearby.

One day Mom wanted to go play at a casino she normally didn't frequent. I was off that day so I took her to where she wanted to go. There was a bunch of 25 cent poker machines against the wall. I set Mom down there and I went to play a little live Texas Hold 'Em.

There is one game in the casino where the house has absolutely no edge. That is the live poker room. The house makes its money in the poker room by taking what's called a rake, or a small percentage of each pot. The house's rake is taken simply to pay for the room, the dealers, the "set up" if you will. When you play live poker you are playing against other players only, not against the house. For this reason and because I just like to play cards, once in a while I'd wander into a low stakes Hold 'Em game.

I came back to check on Mom after I'd played cards for a while. It was about time to go to lunch. There were sixteen machines against the wall and every single one of them was taken. The place was packed. I stood behind Mom and watched her play. The lady on Mom's left swore, grabbed her purse, stood up and walked away.

"Come here Big Dummy," Mom said to me.

"Yea Kid, what's up?" I said. "Ready to go eat?"

"Sit down," Mom said, pointing to the open seat next to her. "Play that machine."

"Mom," I said. "You know I do not play poker machines. I don't play anything but live poker and that only once in a while."

"That machine is gonna hit," Mom said with a tone of complete confidence – no not confidence, absolute surety.

"Mom, nobody knows when a machine is gonna hit. It's all random. This is my business, Kid. I know what I'm talking about."

"Play the machine, it's gonna hit," Mom said again, evidently unimpressed by my vast knowledge of how casinos work.

It was a quarter machine. The most you could bet was five quarters at a time. The biggest payoff was a Royal Flush, which paid $1,100.

"Look Kid," I said, "I don't -."

"You play this machine, it's gonna hit," Mom said again. She did not want to take no for an answer.

"Alright," I said. "If it'll make you happy I'll buy a roll of quarters and play the machine. But $20, that's all I'm gonna play."

"Play the machine, Big Dummy," Mom said as she continued to toss quarters into her machine.

The girl came over and gave me a roll of quarters. I was kinda half scowling when I put the five quarters in, but I said to myself if this makes Mom happy I'll throw $20 away, what the hell.

Five quarters in, I punched the button and was dealt my hand.

A Royal Flush.

The machine went off, all the bells and whistles. Everyone was looking at me and now I'm smilin'. Mom just kept on playing her machine. The girls reset the machine and came back with 11 one hundred dollar bills, which they counted out in my hand.

As soon as the bills were in my hand Mom, who had said not a word to me since the machine hit, now stuck out her left hand towards me, palm up. I put a couple of hundred dollar bills in her hand and just kept going until I got to five hundred bucks. Then Mom closed her hand around the bills and stuck the money in her purse.

Mom wagged her finger at me and said, "From now on you listen to your mom you Big Dummy. Let's go eat."

From then on I listened to my mother when it came to machines. She just had the knack. Almost every time when Mom said play this machine it paid off or when she said stay away from that machine it was ice cold.

There was no science to what Mom did, it was all feel, all intuition. But her calls were far more accurate than just luck. I have no explanation for this, she just had the touch.

Mom once won a $20,000 gift package from a casino – trips, cash, goodies, you name it. She basically supported herself by luck. It was amazing. I wish I had her luck. Maybe it was the Irish in her, who knows, but that lady flat out had the Midas touch.

Mom's friend Sue from Ohio came to town in the late 70s. One morning, we were sitting at Mom's kitchen table after Sue arrived. I'll never forget this conversation…

"So, do you have a job out here Jane?" Sue asked Mom.

"Yep, I work five days a week," Mom answered.

"Where do you work?" Sue asked.

"I get up at six a.m. and go to the Showboat. I play bingo until seven or eight. Then I play video poker machines until nine or so. At ten o'clock I go back to playing bingo. Around eleven, I play the poker machines for another hour. Then I get my free lunch ticket. After lunch, I play bingo or video poker for an hour and then I go home. I never work on Saturday or Sundays," Mom explained.

She was dead serious. Mom didn't get rich with this gambling program, but she came out ahead in the long run. This is not a job I would recommend for anyone, especially and including myself, but it worked for her. Between her gambling winnings, Social Security and pension Mom did more than alright.

**Jimmy's Mom And His Brother Bob**

My mother's maiden name was Jane Conroy. She was a flat out character, an original - full of life and not afraid to stand up for herself. I know that a lot of who I am came from her, and I'm not talking only about genetics. She had a great sense of humor, a big heart and a temper when she was wronged. I learned from an early age that Mom was a pistol…

I went to Central Catholic High School in Canton, Ohio. Prior to my attendance at the school, it once was an all-girls Catholic school called Mt. Marie Academy. My mother went to Mt. Marie Academy.

Jane was a classic tomboy – she was the Captain of her girls' basketball team and she played on the girls' hockey team. Let me put it this way –

Jane Conroy was a nice girl, but she didn't take shit from anybody. That wasn't exactly a popular way for a young lady to conduct herself back in the day, but Mom could have cared less.

When Mom was a high schooler in the 1930s there was a young nun who taught Latin at the Academy. One day this young nun, Sister Berkwin, was droning on and on in her Latin class about her brother. I guess her brother was famous for this and that and the good Sister wanted to share her brother's exploits with the class. Mom, she had another agenda.

"Sister Berkwin," Jane said as she held up her hand.

"Yes, Jane," Sister said, as she called on Mom.

"My father pays good money for me to come to school here. He's not paying you to tell me about your brother, he's paying you to teach me Latin."

The class snickered. Sister Berkwin's face turned red and she stammered for a bit, but she did go back to teaching Latin.

A week or so later, Mom was standing in line at the cafeteria. The rule was that there was no talking in line, but all the girls talked anyway. Sister Berkwin happened to be the lunch monitor that day. Sister walked up to Jane and said sternly, "There is no talking in line, Miss Conroy."

Mom looked around and saw that all the other girls were still yappin' away. Then she said to Sister Berkwin, "When you tell them to be quiet, then I'll shut up." Mom turned her back on Sister Berkwin and kept on talking.

Needless to say, this created some friction between Sister and my mom. Enter young Jimmy Sinay in the 1950s…

Sister Berkwin was 25 years older now, but she was still teaching Latin. I popped into her class as a bright eyed freshman. I remember Mom telling

me about this nun, but she failed to give me any details. So, chipper and anxious to make a good impression I said, "Sister, I believe you taught my mother Latin many years ago."

"Oh?" Sister Berkwin said. "What was your mother's name?"

"Jane Conroy," I answered proudly.

Sister Berkwin's facial expression went from a smile to a frown and then a scowl. What in the world did I say that was so wrong? I wondered. I never got a grade higher than a C- from the good Sister and she treated me like the proverbial red haired step child.

God in heaven, I miss my Mom! She was the best.

# Cindy, the New York Jets and Pinky

Cindy lived down the hall from me at the Patrician Arms. She was a working girl, a prostitute. Cindy was a blast to be around. She had an incredible sense of humor and never took herself too seriously. We never had sex, it was not that kind of relationship. We were buddies and it was great.

I was out one day messin' around and I popped into the College Bowl, a bar I visited on occasion. Cindy was there and boy was she drunk. She started going on about this jerk and that jerk and some guy she was with earlier. I listened to all of her stories. After a while, I said that I was heading home and I offered to give her a ride. Cindy was in no condition to drive, so I took her home.

When we got to Cindy's front door, I fished her key out of her purse and opened the front door. Cindy had this little dog and the dog would bark like crazy if you didn't turn the music on, so I did but real low. I laid Cindy's jacket down on the chair. I put her in bed and covered her up and started to walk out and got to thinkin'… Hmmm… Hmmm…

I'm gonna have a little fun, I said to myself. I reached into her wallet and grabbed a five dollar bill. On Cindy's dresser was a piece of paper and a pen. I wrote this on the paper, "Dear Cindy, What a great time I

had with you last night. That was some good lovin' baby. Here's a little money to say thank you. Signed - ." I scribbled a name down there so you couldn't tell what it was. I put the five dollar bill on top of that piece of paper and set it on the dresser, walked out and went home.

The next morning I'm lying there in bed and I hear pounding on the front door. My roommate got me up and said, "Jim, its Cindy. She's in her robe and she needs to see you now."

So I got up, threw on some clothes and stumbled into the front room.

"Who was I with last night?!" Cindy yelled at me.

"I dunno," I said, keeping a straight face.

"That son of a bitch… that cheap bastard… who was it!"

"Cindy I have no idea what you're talking about," I said.

"Look at this," Cindy said, and then she showed me the note I wrote. "Five dollars! If I find him, I'm gonna kill him."

All day long Cindy was steamin', in fact Cindy was hot for three days about it. Meanwhile, I told my roommate the whole story. He laughed like hell. He thought it was a great joke.

Two weeks later I met this girl. Her name was Barb. She liked to dance, so did I and so one night we went dancing. One thing led to another and I brought her home. I closed the door, we went to bed. It wasn't too late, maybe 11 p.m. or so. We were naked under the sheets making love when all of a sudden the door burst open and the light switched on.

Cindy was standing in my doorway. She had a bag of groceries in her hand and was looking very domestic, not like a working girl.

"You dirty son of a bitch," Cindy said, "here I am working my butt off all night long, slaving away waiting tables to pay our bills. I leave for half an hour to go to the store and what do I come home to? My boyfriend

is in bed in with another woman. How can you do this to me?" Cindy started crying and carrying on.

Barb never said a word. She got outta bed, put on her clothes, grabbed her shoes, walked past Cindy and left. I heard the front door close. Me, I never left the bed.

My roommate suddenly appeared next to Cindy. They started to laugh like hell. Then Cindy said, "Gotcha. That makes us even, Jimmy."

I looked at my roomie and he said to me, "I couldn't help it Jimmy. We had to do it!"

I never did find Barb to tell her that it was all a joke. To this day, she probably thinks I'm the biggest jerk in the world.

♠♦♣♥  ♥♣♦♠

I was at The Flame one afternoon on my day off having a few drinks when my buddy said to me, "You know who that is, Jimmy?"

"No," I said, looking in the direction my buddy was pointing.

"That's Mike Battles from the New York Jets," my buddy said.

"Really?" I said. "Let me buy him a drink." So I did. One thing led to another and Mike Battles and I started talking and swapping stories.

As it turns out, Mike Battles was in town with Tommy McDonald and Joe Namath. Mike said that they were all staying at the Desert Inn. I offered to give Mike a ride back to the DI. We hopped in my car and went to the hotel.

Joe and Tommy were out by the pool. Mike introduced me to Joe and Tommy. What a thrill. I'm a huge football fan and Joe Namath became a legend after the Jets won the Super Bowl in '69. Joe's knees, my God, they were purple. I don't know how the man walked much less played ball.

**Jimmy And Joe Namath**

We all sat by the pool and shot the breeze for an hour or so. I offered to show 'em around Vegas that night and they thought that was a great idea. I called my boss up real quick and got someone to sub for me. I left, cleaned up and came back around seven and picked up the guys. We went and got some dinner.

After eating, we went to the Stardust lounge. There was an act there Joe wanted to see. We sat in a booth in the back of the lounge. It wasn't long before a group of people, I guess there were seven or eight of 'em, stopped by the table with paper and pens and wanted to get Joe's autograph. Tommy and Mike signed for them too.

Somebody stuck a pen and paper in front of me. Joe was sitting to my right. I said to Joe, "Look! They want my autograph. A craps dealer."

"Sign it Don Maynard," Namath said. "I'll tell Don. He'll get a big kick out of it."

So I signed Don Maynard on a couple of pieces of paper.

I had a great time with Joe, Tommy and Mike that night. We screwed around and laughed and let loose. They were regular guys and treated me like I was one of their circle of friends.

The Chateau Vegas was a bar that was about a hundred feet away from my apartment complex. I liked going to the Chateau because I could hang out, have a few drinks, or a few too many drinks, and then just walk home.

In the 70s, my friends and I tried not to drink and drive. Nowadays, I guess the sobriety behind the wheel movement really got going in the 80s, we all know better than to drink and drive. Thank the Good Lord above, in the old days I never got a DUI or hurt myself or anybody else driving my car after I'd had a few. Back then, people didn't look at drinking and driving the same way as they do now. Anyway, I tried to never get behind the wheel after drinking too much.

One night after making the rounds I ended up back at the Chateau. My buddy was tending bar, so if nothing else was happening I could always go to the Chateau, sit around and shoot the breeze. When I walked in the Chateau that night, I immediately noticed this gorgeous redhead at the bar. She wasn't with anyone and there wasn't a ring on her finger. I was pretty good at spotting working girls and this lady was definitely not a working girl. So I said hi and bought her a drink. Then I made my move.

"What's the chances of us goin' out?" I asked her.

"Not too good," she said.

"What's the chances of us exchanging phone numbers?" I asked.

"Not too good," she said again.

I was feeling frisky and decided to go for it. "What's the chances of us going back to my place and having sex all night long?"

She reached over, grabbed me by the collar and punched me in the chest as hard as she could. I slipped off the bar stool and grabbed the bar with my left hand so I didn't completely fall to the floor. That lady had some strength!

Hanging there, trying not to fall to the floor, I managed to eke out, "So I guess a blow job is out of the question."

That did it. The beautiful lady was completely disarmed. She started laughing and helped me back on my stool. I'd broken the ice and made a friend.

For the next hour, she told me about how she had just caught her boyfriend fooling around with another woman, how mad she was, blah, blah, blah. She was a waitress at a casino. We had a couple more drinks. She was a really nice person going through a rough time.

She stayed with me for the next two days. She needed someone to help her get over her old boyfriend. I was the perfect medicine to heal her broken heart.

Pinky was the valet parker at the Chateau. After a few years he valeted at Caesar's and at some other joints too. Back in the day, a guy could make some dough parking cars. Say you parked 50 cars a night and got

an average tip of a buck and a half, that's $75 a shift. Not bad money in the 1970s.

I loved Pinky. Truly a nice man, but he had one fatal flaw. Every time he put some money together, a few grand, he took it all and gambled it on a crap game. What Pinky wanted to do more than anything else was open up a little bar/restaurant back in the Midwest. He needed $40,000 to do that. But rather than waiting five or six years to save up the dough, Pinky thought the best way to get what he needed was to take $4,000 to a craps table and get lucky.

I've seen this kinda thing a bunch of times. It seems so easy, in theory. Put $4,000 on the pass line. Roll seven or make your number. Now you've got $8,000. Let it ride and win again. Now you've got $16,000. Let it ride once more and you're up $32,000. One more time and you're a $60,000 winner. Four passes in a row. I've seen the dice pass as much as twenty times in a row, but that's very rare. Usually the dice pass once or twice, then the shooter seven's out.

Gambling is not the way to make money. Can you get lucky? Sure, that's possible but the odds are that you'll lose. Pinky was no exception, he was the rule. Time after time, when he'd save two or three or four grand he'd shoot craps and lose.

Eventually, Pinky got around to playing craps at the Tropicana. The Trop had a $5,000 limit with $10,000 odds. That's the most you could bet without getting permission from the house. This time Pinky broke his losing trend, he started winning. He pushed the bet higher and higher and he kept winning.

He had money on the six, eight, nine and the pass line - about $20,000 on the table. This was his big moment. If he could roll a ten before he

rolled a seven, Pinky would have all the money he needed to open up his bar. He blew on the dice, said a prayer and tossed the dice across the table.

One die came a six, the other one spun around and eventually it settled on… one. Seven out. Pinky lost again.

Pinky went home in his little pink VW Bug that night saying to himself, "I can get 'em next time. I was so close. Next time for sure." Well, he never did "get 'em". Vegas got Pinky. He never left town and a few years after that night at the Trop Pinky got a bad drug habit, the hard stuff. It eventually killed him in the 1990s.

For every winner story, there are fifty loser stories. I'm amazed that people don't understand basic math. The casinos sure do. That's why they make millions of dollars, year in and year out.

# The Bachelor Book and the Great Chip Robbery

My friend Liz Gini asked me one day if I wanted to be part of a book she was writing called, *The Bachelor Book*. Her goal was to introduce the ladies to the most eligible bachelors in Vegas back in the day. Remember, in the 70s and 80s there was no social media and no internet dating. Everything was done the old fashioned way. As it turns out, Liz was on to something. She not only wrote *The Bachelor Book*, but she followed that up with a *Bachelorette Book* featuring women.

I…ahem…ahem… was the first man profiled in *The Bachelor Book*. Just look at my young self! Yea, I was channeling my inner Tom Selleck, that's for sure! Liz was really cute in what she had to say about me….

*"It would be worth a crick in your neck to be able to keep looking up at this bachelor. This gorgeous, intelligent man has chosen to live a low keyed, un-hassled life in this glamorous city. Jim is a dealer at one of the Strip hotels. He drinks alcohol moderately, uses no drugs and stays in excellent shape with weights, tennis and basketball."*

Well, Liz got most of that right. I'm not sure about the "low keyed and un-hassled life" comment but, oh well. Liz went on to say…

**Liz Gini**

> "This man's friends think the world of him. He goes along with the crowd, but because he is an individualist, conducts himself independently. He is highly regarded by his friends because of his consistent honesty, his ability to be a good listener and a good friend."

> "Women describe this gentleman as very attractive, warm and refreshingly colorful. Although he is bright, Jim admits, 'I do occasionally get crabby'."

> "He is attracted to women in the 25 to 40 range because they know what they want and what they don't want. He takes care in selecting sophisticated, first class ladies with whom to share his time; ladies who have a genuineness."

> "Physical attributes he finds most appealing are waist, tush, legs, face and hair."

Gee that about covers it doesn't it? What else is there? I mean at least I didn't mention the only missing ingredient in that recipe, breasts! Speaking of recipes…

> "Jim is such an excellent cook that ladies become apprehensive about returning the gesture. 'It's not fair' says Jim. So, if you'd like to make an impression, at least throw together some hors d'oeuvres."

I look back on that book now and I laugh. That sort of thing is commonplace today – pull up any Facebook post. But in 1980, unless you were a celebrity blowing your own horn in public wasn't normally done. Did I get some dates from being in Liz's book? Yea, no doubt. More importantly I made a good friend. Liz Gini and I remain friends to this day.

In the 1970s there was a rather infamous incident that involved a man whose job it was to take checks, in this story I call them casino "chips", collected at the Desert Inn from other casinos and cash them in. Every casino honored every other casino's chips so if you were gambling at the Sahara and you had Dunes chips, you could just lay those Dunes chips down and play. Every so often someone from the casino would collect all the chips from the other joints and go to each place and cash them in.

Well, one day this man put all of the chips from the other casinos that the Desert Inn collected over a considerable period of time into his van. His job was to stop at the casinos, exchange the chips for cash and then bring the cash back to the Desert Inn. This time the man collected all the money, but he never returned to the Desert Inn. A few months later the stolen van was recovered in Florida. They never did catch the guy, at least as far as I know.

A few weeks later two yokels, a couple of losers with less brains than the average hamster, heard about this great chip robbery. They thought to themselves, Hmmm… maybe we could get away with this caper too!

They were milling around in the back of a casino one day when they saw a white van pull up and park at the rear loading dock. On the side of the van in big letters was written "Las Vegas Chips". They could not get close enough to see what was going on, but they did see people loading and unloading boxes from the van. The geniuses said to each other, "Boxes of chips!" So they not so carefully planned their heist.

Their criminal plan was simple – follow the van around town and when it looked to them like it had made enough stops, find a way to strong arm the driver and steal all the chips. So that's what they did. They kept a fair distance back, because they thought the van was making the rounds

collecting chips. They watched and waited and looked for just the right moment.

Then the wanna be evil masterminds caught a break. The van turned down a side street away from the casinos. Now was the time. They swerved in front of the van and forced it to pull off the road. They pointed guns at the driver who immediately complied with their demand to get out of the van and take a hike.

Seeing that the coast was clear, Frick and Frack approached the rear door. They wondered if they would have to break through a heavy lock or maybe shoot their way in. Was there another guard, armed to the teeth, just waiting for them inside? They did think it was odd that the man they chased away had a "Vegas Chips" uniform shirt on, but he was not armed. They thought maybe the casinos just wanted to keep the whole operation low key so no one could find out about it and rob them. Yea, that had to be it.

The rear door was unlocked, so the thieves opened it with no problem. Inside were twenty or so boxes marked, "Vegas Chips". It was time to get paid! They took another look around and there was still no one nearby so they opened one of the boxes expecting to see a small fortune in front of them.

The box was full of chips alright. As were all the other boxes. Only not casino chips, potato chips. "Vegas Chips" was a brand name used by a chip manufacturer to try and make a dent in the lucrative Las Vegas food service biz.

Next thing you know a couple of squad cars come roaring up the alley. The delivery driver had called the cops. Imagine that 911 exchange, "I drive a potato chip truck and I've just been robbed at gunpoint". The two

schmucks got hauled away in cuffs but not before the cops had a belly laugh. What an episode.

There have been movies made about people who supposedly figured out a way to successfully rob a casino. *Ocean's 11* comes to mind. Back in the day when the boys ran the town such things were possible on a small scale. One group of guys taking from another group of guys, etc. Once the corporations took over Las Vegas, security got tighter than Fort Knox. There will always be the "snatch and run" type penny ante stuff, but taking down the vault at a Las Vegas casino?

If you've got that kind of ambition, you better bring an army, because they'll be an army waiting for you. In my opinion, you can put all those Hollywood fantasies in the next to impossible to pull off category.

# The Silverbird, Redd Foxx and Dancing with Debbie

As with many things in life, what appears at first to be a setback is often really a step up. That was definitely the case in terms of my termination from the Sahara. A friend of mine was an exec at the Silverbird. When he found out that I was unemployed, he asked me if I wanted to run their dice pit, to become a floor supervisor. That sounded good to me.

One of the people I remember most from the Silverbird days was the comedian/actor Redd Foxx. Most people remember Redd from his hit TV show *Sanford and Son*, but I liked him best as a standup comedian. Man was that guy funny.

Redd liked to play blackjack and keno. He always had a huge stack of Keno tickets sitting by him at the blackjack table. Redd played multiple tickets on every game. It took two Keno runners to add up all his tickets, figure out how much he had won or lost, and then ask him which tickets he wanted to play the next game.

Now that I was a boss, I had the freedom to move around the casino so once in a while I made my way over to where Redd was sitting and we talked. His wife was a nice lady and she loved playing the poker machines and keno. Many nights I just hung out with Redd and listened

to him tell stories about his television show and the people he knew in the entertainment industry. He was a joy to be around.

We had this security guard at the Silverbird who wanted desperately to be a cop. I'm not sure exactly why, but he was turned down by Metro (Las Vegas police) to become an officer on more than one occasion. Maybe it was because he was such an "eager beaver", to use an old expression. This guy was always looking for some way to exert authority over someone else. So, of course, I was always looking for some way to play a joke on him.

One week we had a convention of deaf mute people at the Bird. They communicated with each other using sign language and by reading each other's lips. I saw that a group of ten of these fine deaf mute folks were congregated in front of the dice pit all yapping away with their hands. So I got this great idea…

I looked for the security guard and I saw him in the twenty one area. I motioned for him to come see me. He came right over to where I was standing.

"Yes sir," the security guard said.

"See that group of people over there?" I said, pointing to the group of deaf mutes.

"Yes sir," the security guard said, now giving the bunch his best evil eye.

"I have told those people now three times, there is no singing in here. They keep doing it. They just don't care what I tell them or what the rules are. Go over and tell 'em to stop."

"Yes sir," the security guard said.

This fellow went over to the circle of deaf mutes and tapped one of them on the shoulder. I'm watching this from thirty feet away trying my best to keep a straight face. The guard was truly confused for a minute – he didn't get it right away that these good folks were incapable of speech, much less singing.

With a confused look on his face, he looked back at me and then back at them and then back at me. I couldn't take it anymore. I bust out laughing. So did a few of the other people in the dice pit. The guard's face turned as red as an apple and he walked away.

Later on, I caught up with the guard and made peace. I told him I just couldn't help myself and that I hoped he saw the humor in what I'd done. Plenty of times guys pulled jokes on me, it's just what we did. After a few minutes, I got him to laugh about it too.

♠♦♣♥  ♥♣♦♠

Linda, a cocktail waitress at the Hilton, and I went out for a while. Notice that I dated a lot of cocktail waitresses? That was pretty natural because that's where Vegas people met other people to date, at work. Plus all the little bars and restaurants I frequented were also frequented by people who worked at the casinos. I simply didn't get the chance to meet many teachers or nurses, etc.

There was a lounge at the Hilton where Little Richard was performing. Linda got off around two a.m. One night the plan was for me to meet her at this lounge after she got off. I got to the lounge and sat in the back, well away from the stage. I was by myself.

Little Richard was maybe fifty feet away from me pounding away on the keyboard. Then a couple of his band members came out in the crowd

and they started getting people up to dance. They were doing a "snake dance" - everyone formed a line, boy-girl, boy-girl, etc. and they were dancing around the lounge.

I was just sipping a drink and waiting for Linda. I love to dance, but that night I wasn't at all interested in doing the snake dance. The snake passed me by and I just sat there. Then I felt a tap on my shoulder.

"Get up and dance," a voice behind me said. I could tell it was female, but I didn't know who it was.

"Nah," I said, only halfway turning around, "I'm fine right here."

"Why don't you get up and dance?" the lady behind me urged me again.

I had to see who was pestering me to dance, so I turned around completely. It was Debbie Reynolds, the famous actress and singer.

"With you, I'll dance," I said.

So I got up, put my hands on her hips and we snaked danced down to the main floor.

"Can you swing dance?" Debbie asked me.

"I used to enter swing dance contests," I told Debbie.

Debbie and I started swing dancing to Little Richard. The snake dance people formed a big circle around us. We were having a ball. I'm a good West Coast swing dancer. When the song was over everybody applauded us. I walked Debbie over to her table.

"You know something?" Debbie said to me. "When you get off your dead ass you do a helluva job on the dance floor."

I gave her a hug, a kiss on the cheek and I said, "Debbie, you're the best."

Linda showed up right after that and we went out and had a good time. Every time I went in there after that, the cocktail waitresses would bust my chops and ask me if I was gonna dance with Debbie tonight.

# It Wasn't All Fun and Games

I went to this little place called the Coachman's down on Eastern and DI once in a while. The food was good and I knew a lot of people who went there. They had a nice fireplace and Christmas tree that they kept up year round. My buddy Chicky Rudifino and I ended up goin' in there when we were out and about together.

It was early evening and Chicky and I saw a cocktail waitress friend of ours and some guy I had never met before. The cocktail waitress said hello and she asked us if we would like to join them. As always, I said yes. I'm a friendly guy and there is really nothing I like more than meeting new people.

We all sat down together and ordered drinks. The guy with this cocktail waitress friend of ours didn't say a word. He had a plateful of food and he was chowin' down.

Now, as you might expect, when three people who all work in the same joint all get together we all started talking about what happened at the casino that week. I chimed in on a couple of subjects – we were all just shootin' the breeze.

Out of nowhere this guy says to me, "You don't know what the fuck you're talking about. You're an asshole. I can tell assholes when I see 'em."

I set my drink down, looked at this guy and said, "What did you say?"

He said, "You heard me you son of a bitch. I don't like you." Then he picked up the knife he'd been eating with and tried to stab me with it.

I grabbed this guy's wrist, turned it and the knife dropped. Then I punched him in the nose. It wasn't some "hello, nice to see ya" punch, I nailed the guy. Blood started flowing.

I dragged this man from the booth and as I'm dragging him across the floor I'm hitting him with my elbow and my knee. I'm trying to snap this asshole's arm off. I get him over to the fireplace. I started to shove him into the fireplace, which was on at the time.

Have I mentioned that it was just not a good idea to screw with me back in the day? I wasn't the toughest customer in the world, but I know how to handle myself. Years playing sports and few more in the military taught me some self-defense skills.

The bartender and Chicky came runnin' over and stopped me. "Jim, you're killin' this guy," Chicky said. "You need to leave him alone. The cops are on their way. Get the hell off of him."

So I just dropped the dude on the floor. The bartender said, "Jim, get out of here. I'll take care of the cops. That idiot pulled a knife on you, I'll tell 'em you were just protecting yourself."

Later Chicky told me that the bartender threw the guy out of the place right after I left and told him never to come back. By the time the cops got there they didn't have anything to go on because "nobody saw nothin'".

A week later I went to get in my car to go to work. All my tires were flat. There were holes in 'em; somebody had punctured all four of my Goodyear radials. I called AAA, they came out and took my Caddy to the garage. I got four new tires put on the car. I told all my neighbors to watch out, to look for anybody strange walking around the complex.

It wasn't long after that when one day after work I noticed that the trunk of my car had acid thrown on it. I said, that's it. I got the Caddy's paint fixed. Then I went to the cocktail waitress and asked for this asshole's name and where he worked. I found out where he liked to hang out. Turns out he came in the Chateau once in a while.

I told the guys tending bar down at the Chateau, all of whom were friends of mine, "You know so and so. When he comes in here, you call me." They all agreed to do that for me, no problem.

A few days later I had some people over at my place. I saw this car moving slowly down the alley. I saw a guy get out. It was him. I went running down the stairs (I lived on the second and third floors of my building) and saw that this fool had light bulbs full of acid in his hands. He tossed one of these things at me and the bulb hit the cement and exploded.

He got in his car, but the only way to get back on Desert Inn Road was to go right past me. I was standing smack dab in the middle of the alley. He floored it, but I had to get out of the way. There is no way I could tussle with a two thousand pound car. As the idiot drove off I said to myself, I'm gonna get that guy sooner or later.

About a week later I got a phone call from the Chateau Vegas. One of my friends told me the guy I was looking for was in the place.

I walked in the Chateau and there he was sitting on the end of the bar. I picked him up and slammed him against the wall three or four times. Then I hit him in the mouth. I dragged him to the corner and said to him in front of a bunch of witnesses, "If you ever screw with me, my friends or my property I'll bury you alive. You little son of a bitch, I'll bury your fuckin' ass alive." Then I threw him against the wall.

He sat there looking at me. I stood over him and made damn sure this fool knew that I was as serious as cancer. Then I went home.

A few weeks later I got a knock on my door. I got up and answered it. It was a police officer. The cop wanted to talk to me. I showed him in and we sat down.

"I understand that you had a confrontation with so and so," the cop said.

"Yea, sure did. He pulled a knife on me, cut my tires and threw acid on my car," I said. I had nothin' to hide. It's not like plenty of people didn't know all this already.

"We found him… He's dead," the cop said.

"What?" I said.

"He's dead." The cop described where they found the guy by Sunrise Mountain on the east side of town.

"Wow. I had nothin' to do with it," I said. Then the cop asked me where I was at certain hours the day before. I was lucky. I had been at work all day long. I told him who to call to verify my alibi.

Later on, I found out through a cop buddy that this bozo was having sex with a drug dealer's girlfriend. This drug dealer offered a cash reward to anybody who did this guy in. All of this had nothing to do with me, but that's why the cops came sniffing around my apartment.

To this day, I have no idea why this clown came after me. Vegas had a few of these types, people with no common sense or self-control. What's the old saying? There is nothing more dangerous than a crazy person? There's a certain amount of truth in that.

Some friends of mine bought a small gold mine down in Wickenburg, Arizona. They wanted to know if I wanted to invest in the mine. It wasn't a large cash outlay, only $500, but I also had to do my share of the work. What the hell, I said. So I got a thirty day leave of absence from my job. Hey, how often do you get the chance to work in your own gold mine?

I left my car in Wickenburg at a friend's house. I did not want to be driving my caddy through the open desert. My friend, one of the co-owners of the mine, had an old pick-up truck. There were four of us set to work the mine for the next month. I had my thirty eight pistol strapped to my hip with snake shot in it. There were a lot of snakes down there and I do not like snakes of any kind.

We headed for the gold mine. We traveled on more of a trail than a road. It took us three plus hours to get from Wickenburg to the gold mine. It was literally out in the middle of nowhere. When we arrived, I noticed a small cabin and a tent. That's where we were to stay at night. The entrance to the mine was fifty feet away from the cabin.

The second day we were there we discovered that we needed to get one of our drills repaired. The closest place we could get a drill repaired was from a group of people who lived a few miles away. These folks lived in a commune of some sort, or so I was told. So we all piled into the truck and headed for this commune.

While it wasn't very far as the crow flies, it took us over an hour to get over there. This place was way back in the hills. They had a substantial set-up. There were a lot of buildings; to me it looked a lot like a Midwest farm. There were maybe a hundred people living in this compound. My buddies said that these folks just wanted to live off away from everyone else and do their own thing. They had pigs, cows, chickens – the entire

operation was basically self-sustaining. They grew crops. There was a stream that ran through their property. They had a generator of some sort that supplied electric power. I was told that a few of the guys who lived there had jobs in the city and brought the money back to the commune. That's how they got the dough for extra supplies.

Every man walking around the commune was packing heat. That made me a bit nervous. Why was everybody armed? I told my buddy that going to a place where everyone wore a gun on their hip might not be a good idea. I was reassured that these people were okay, they're just into themselves, they're harmless, etc.

They fixed our drill in fairly short order and we paid them for it. They invited us to stay for supper. Before the meal was served everyone stood and offered a prayer. Not a scrap of food was wasted, every plate was completely cleaned. Reminded me of stories I'd heard about the Great Depression. These folks were a frugal bunch.

After dinner, a couple of guys invited us to shoot guns with them. They were having some sort of contest. I took aim at the pistol target and fired. I missed! Now I'm a very good shot and I couldn't understand this, but then my brain kicked in and reminded me that I had snake shot in my pistol. Snake shot is like turning your pistol into a small scatter gun. It's designed to kill snakes, not hit targets. The guys from the commune thought that was funny, but I just put my gun away and didn't say another word.

When we hopped into the truck to leave, the weather started changing. It got dark and windy and cold. We got part of the way back to the cabin when the sky just opened up. It was raining in sheets. Now I've seen my share of heavy rain back in Ohio and in Asia, but this was something else.

You could not see five feet in front of the truck. Mud was everywhere. The trail we were following basically disappeared. The truck was slipping all over the place. I was praying that we would make it back to the mine in one piece.

We got within fifty yards of the mine when the truck started to slide sideways. I was riding in the back bed of the truck, keeping dry under a tarp. There was a twenty foot drop off to my right and the truck was headed that way! So I stood up and I was about to jump out of the truck when the truck hit a huge bump and tossed me out. Sitting there in the mud I looked up and the truck was headed straight for me! I tried to get up, but I was stuck! A few feet before I got run over, the truck somehow stopped, just inches short of going over the hill and falling twenty feet to the bottom of a gulley.

What the hell were we supposed to do now? The truck was stuck in the mud and the rain was pouring down. One of the guys said that we had to go back into Wickenburg and get a small tractor he had stashed and drive it back to the mine. The only way back to Wickenburg now was to walk. There was no way we were going to move the truck even one inch without a winch.

I was in better shape than two of the other guys so I volunteered to hoof it. The other guy who went with me was a 21 year old kid. This kid had the keys to the tractor. So I said, "Let's go pal." It was maybe 40 degrees outside and it was wet. I was not a happy little miner.

We left around eight o'clock at night. We had a couple of hours of daylight left and the rain had let up a bit, but it was still coming down. We walked maybe three hours or so, it was dark outside and we stopped to rest.

"Did you see that on the hill up there?" the kid said to me.

"What?" I asked.

"Those green eyes," the kid said. "That's a mountain lion. He's following us so be careful."

I reached in my pocket and switched out my snake shot shells for standard shells. If that damn mountain lion came near me, I'd have to shoot him.

The rain picked up again. We kept walking. We were soaked to the bone. It was dark and it was cold. I wanted to sit and rest, but the kid kept saying that we had to keep moving. He was afraid that if we sat and got stiff, the lion would take that as a sign of weakness and pounce on us. So we kept walking.

Around four in the morning I had to stop. It was still raining. I was in my thirties and in decent shape, but I was completely exhausted. I looked in front of me and I was staring right into the eyes of that mountain lion. He could not have been thirty feet away from me. I started to tell that kid that I was spent, that he needed to go on ahead of me and bring back some help.

I was doubled over, trying to catch my breath. I looked on the ground near my feet. On the ground was a newspaper. The headline read, "Jim Sinay Dies in Desert Because He Quit".

I blinked my eyes. The newspaper was gone.

I said to the kid, "Let's go. Nobody's gonna say Jim Sinay died in the desert because he quit." No matter what, now I was determined not to stop. I was making it on pure adrenaline alone.

We got maybe twenty yards when I heard a growling type sound behind us. The mountain lion was creeping towards us, ready to attack. Both the

kid and I fired at that lion and we put him down right there in the mud. That made me sad, the lion was a beautiful creature, but it was him or me. I did not want to be that lion's breakfast.

We kept on walking. Our hope and prayer was that there was not another mountain lion around because we only had a couple of shells left.

Around seven a.m., we got back to Wickenburg. I went straight to a motel. The kid went back to his house, took a nap and got the tractor. After a few hours, the kid came by the motel to get me, but I told him that I was going back to the casinos. My $500 investment wasn't worth getting killed over. He said he understood and wished me well.

When I say that I saw that newspaper, I mean I saw that damn newspaper. I would gladly swear to that on a stack of Bibles. I was ready to give up and if I had, who knows what might have happened. I could easily have been mountain lion food.

I went back to Vegas, started working again and thanked God for sparing my life.

# Felicia Atkins and Showgirl Island

I was out and about one evening and having a drink in a bar. When I looked to my right, I saw this absolutely stunning woman. She was five ten or so, black hair and green eyes. This lady wasn't pretty, she was drop dead gorgeous. So of course I'm going to say hello.

Now, I had no way of knowing this, but Felicia Atkins was at one time a Playboy centerfold. She was Miss April 1958. Felicia was also the lead showgirl at the Tropicana Hotel in the Follies Bergere. We got to talking and I soon discovered that this beautiful woman was also a very nice person. I asked her out and we decided to have a bite to eat the next night after work.

We went on our date, a two in the morning date, to this place on the Strip called The Leaning Tower of Pizza. It was familiar ground to the locals and was best known as an afterhours joint. Frank Sinatra and his crowd were regulars in there.

Felicia didn't have time to take off her showgirl makeup. Now, there is a big difference between a showgirl and a dancer. A showgirl performed in a line with other showgirls and wore elaborate costumes. Being a dancer could mean a variety of things, but dancers were not showgirls. For one thing, to be a showgirl you had to be tall, five feet nine or taller.

If you were small in stature you could not wear the elaborate costumes appropriately, especially the headgear which could weigh as much as ten pounds or more. Also, you had to have a nice figure and be comfortable showing your breasts. The first show the showgirls kept their tops on. For the late show they went topless.

Felicia and I walked into the Leaning Tower of Pizza. There were only a few other people in there at the time. There was this man who was facing us and he was with a woman, his wife or date I presume. Her back was turned to us. When he saw Felicia he was about to take a bite of his spaghetti, but the pasta never reached his mouth. His eyes got wide and he just sat there, mouth wide open, staring at Felicia as she walked past.

The lady he was sitting with saw what he was doing. She picked up the plate of spaghetti in front of her and dumped it on his head. She stood up and walked out.

There were some people I knew sitting in the back so we joined them. Then some more friends of mine stopped by so before long we had a little party going.

Felicia and I dated a few more times. She was such a nice, classy woman. She told me one day, "Jimmy, this is my year for a bullfighter". I said, "Honey you have a great time." She dated this famous bullfighter for a while. Unfortunately, I lost track of Felicia in the 1980s. She was Australian and I was told that she went back to Australia and is living there now.

In the 1970s, when you got off the airplane at McCarran Airport one of the first things you saw was a huge billboard with Felicia on it in her full showgirl costume. Her picture was truly an iconic image of old Vegas. In the 1990s, they had a reunion of the showgirls from the Tropicana, the

Dunes all the joints that had the big productions. They defined the "ideal showgirl". Who was it? Felicia, of course. She was perfection.

♠♦♣♥    ♥♣♦♠

Lake Mead, the body of water created by Hoover Dam, is just to the south of Las Vegas. The lake is huge – it extends about a hundred miles from the dam back towards the Grand Canyon. The lake contains enough water to cover the entire state of Pennsylvania in a foot of water.

Because it gets and stays hot in the desert from May through October, the water temperature in Lake Mead is in the high 80s. Boating on the lake is a blast, but when it's 110 degrees outside you get fried quickly.

One of the first times I went to the lake was with a dealer buddy of mine in the early 1970s. I'd never been on the lake before. Now, truth be told, Lake Mead isn't the most scenic place unless you like the desert. Everything is grey and dusty and rocky. Not too many trees and nothing but scrub vegetation.

"Where we goin'?" I asked my buddy as I climbed into his boat. What the hell was there to look at out here? I said in my mind. Didn't seem to be too much to view other than rocks and sand.

"You'll see," he said, grinning at me.

My friend piloted his boat away from the marina headed northeast (away from the Dam). Maybe half an hour later or so we got to this island. From a distance, it looked like everything else out here, a bunch of dirty boulders and dusty ground sticking up out of the water.

But, oh baby, this island was anything but boring.

We circled the island and I saw a lot of people. Ninety percent of them were women and all of them were topless!

"What's goin' on here?" I said. Suddenly I was in love with Lake Mead.

"This is where the showgirls come to sunbathe. It's like their little hangout. You can't get here unless you've got a boat. There's a bunch of cocktail waitresses over there too. They don't want lines showing when they wear their uniforms or costumes."

We went around the island a couple of times and then pulled the boat up to the landing spot on the beach. We got out and walked around. There were topless women everywhere! We sat down and just took in the whole scene.

"We gotta get out of here," I told my friend.

"Why? Don't you like it here?" he asked.

"Like it here… My God, I love this place. It's driving me nuts though. All these beautiful women topless. It's too much!" I said.

My buddy laughed. We got back in his boat and took off. We didn't go straight back to the marina though, we headed towards the Dam. My buddy had a pal that he wanted me to meet. I said okay. My head was still swimming with images of women's breasts all bouncing in front of me…

We pulled up next to a boat that was floating in front of the Dam. Hoover Dam is really impressive when you see it up close and personal from the water. There was a guy in the boat and he was putting on scuba gear.

"Where you goin'?" I asked the guy as we pulled up next to his boat.

"I inspect the Dam for the State of Nevada. I look for cracks and other problems," he said.

"I used to be a diver down in Florida," I told the guy.

"Oh yea. See some big fish in Florida?" he asked me as he kept putting on his gear.

"Swam with some sharks from time to time," I said.

"Well, down there," he said, pointing at the dark blue water in front of the Dam, "are some of the biggest catfishes on the planet. I run into some scary beasts – six foot long catfish with a mouthful of really nasty teeth."

"You're kidding," I said.

"I do my inspection, but I keep one eye on the catfish. I give those suckers plenty of room. Gotta go."

The guy jumped in the lake and my buddy and I went back to the marina.

Lake Mead is too hot and too barren to be attractive to me so I didn't spend a whole lot of time there, but I have to tell ya that my vision of heaven has to include Showgirl Island. What a place.

# The Kinky Stuff

If you had to describe me in terms of my sexual preferences, I would say that I'm 100% heterosexual male. I'm not much for anything too ambitious or wild, but I do like the ladies. One on one in private, that's my style. I'm not a big fan of porn, but once in a while looking at a picture of Playboy bunny or a topless showgirl, that's alright with me.

Vegas these days is known for its wild sex side. You've got topless clubs, sex clubs, cat houses (north of the city) and any type of hooker you could possibly imagine is yours for the asking through any one of a thousand escort services. Back in the day, 30 or 40 years ago, it was the same, only much more low key.

There was this bar on Paradise Road called Black Magic. I'd never been in the place, but I'd driven by it a hundred times. So one night I said, what the hell. Let's check it out.

I went up to the bar and ordered a drink. The bartender brought me a beer. I sat there for a while sipping my beer and minding my own business. There was a dance floor – no live music but I could tell that people danced here to tapes and records. Around this dance floor were booths.

In the booths I saw three or four girls sitting together, then there were two guys in another, then a few girls all crammed into another. These people are afraid to mix it up, I thought to myself. Bunch of shy folks.

After I had drunk the beer, I had to pee so I asked the bartender where the men's room was. He told me to go down to the end of the bar and take a right and it was right there. So I got up and went to the restroom.

I was standing at the urinal relieving myself when a guy walked in. He stood to my right and said, "Would you like someone to help you hold that?"

"What did you say?" I asked.

"Would you like me to help you hold that?"

I looked at him and said, "Get your ass outta here right now."

"No problem," he said and then he left.

As I was washing my hands I said to myself, what the hell was all that? Some guy coming on to me in the restroom? Do I look gay? Why the hell would he do that?

I sat back down at the bar and the bartender came over to see if I wanted another beer. I said that I did and then I said, "You won't believe what happened to me in that bathroom a couple of minutes ago."

"Oh yeah… I already know," he said.

"Whaddya mean?" I said.

"Word is already around. You're straight."

"I don't get it," I said.

"This is your first time in here, isn't it?" he asked.

"Yea, so," I said.

"Look around. Look on the dance floor."

I did. On the dance floor, two pairs of guys were dancing with each other and four girls were dancing together. It was a gay bar. Me, Big Dummy, the dimmest bulb in the box, was clueless.

"Nobody will bother you now that they know you're straight. It's cool," the bartender said.

I downed my beer and left. I never went back in that bar, it closed a few months later. These days our culture says that being gay is alright. You can even get married now to another person of your same sex. Back in the 70s though that wasn't the case.

As for me, I've always had the philosophy that people should basically be left the hell alone to do what they want to do as long as they aren't hurting anyone else. Long before it was the popular thing to do or say, I was a live and let live type guy. Never gave the whole gay or straight thing a whole lot of thought really. I think everyone deserves to be treated with respect.

♠♦♣♥ ♥♣♦♠

There was a hotel on the south end of the Strip, back in the day it was the last place on the Strip going south, called the Hacienda. My buddy Hal gave me a call one day and said to me, "Jimmy, they've got a new swingers club down at the Hacienda. We should go check it out."

"Great. Tomorrow?" I said.

"You're on, Jim," Hal said.

Hal and I shared a passion for swing dancing. Not a lot of places back in the day featured swing dancing so when Hal heard the Hacienda was sponsoring a club he immediately thought of me.

I put on a nice pair of shoes and slacks that night. I was really excited. I used to enter swing dance contests in California and I loved it. I picked Hal up and off we went.

The swinger's event was held in a convention type room at the hotel. As we walked in I told Hal, "Man, some of these women here are gorgeous!" Everyone seemed to be paired up with someone else, which wasn't unusual. A lot of couples like to swing dance.

We got in the place and were just standing there when this good looking lady and her husband, I assumed from the wedding rings, approached us.

"Hi," she said. "I'm Cherry. This is Ken."

Hal and I introduced ourselves and then Cherry said, "Are you guys gay?"

"Whaddya mean?" I asked.

"Are you gay?" Cherry asked again.

"No, we're straight" I said, now totally confused. What the hell does being gay or straight have to do with swing dancing?

"Oh, okay," Cherry said. She turned around and started to walk away when Ken touched her arm and whispered in her ear. Then she turned back to me and asked, "Would you like to swing with us?"

"Hmmm…" I said. "You're talkin' about swing dancing, in a contest?"

Cherry looked at Ken, then she looked at Hal and then she and Ken busted up laughing. After a minute she said to me, "Do you know where you are?"

"Yea. Isn't this a swing dance club?" I said.

"No, this is a swing association. We swing with other partners. Sex," Cherry said.

"Oh…" I said, my face now turning a deep shade of red. "Oh… I … oh."

"It's too bad you're not here with a girl," Cherry said. "Ken and I would have enjoyed that."

"Well, thanks anyway," I said. Hal and I turned and left as quickly as we could.

When we got to the parking lot, I said to Hal, "I hope nobody that works in the casinos saw us in there. They'd get the wrong idea."

We laughed. Another Vegas experience, another hilarious memory.

# Bomberas, Baccarat Dealers and Tony

One of the best restaurants back in the day in Vegas was a place called Bomberas. It was up near Sunrise Mountain on East Charleston. It was an old house that had been converted into a restaurant. Carlo Bombera and his wife Mary owned the establishment.

You had to have reservations to go there and eat. Why? The Bomberas only cooked one meal per night. There was no menu. Whatever they were cooking, that's what was served. Unless Carlo knew exactly how many people were coming, he could not figure out how much food to make.

You could call a day or two in advance to see what Carlo and Mary were making on a particular night. Carlo had a sign up in the main dining room that read, "If You Don't Like Garlic, Go Home." He meant it too. They served absolutely extraordinary Italian cuisine. Even today, I can close my eyes and smell the incredible veal dish they made, taste the always fresh pasta and savor the antipasto appetizers. Bomberas served the best Italian food I've ever had and I've had plenty.

One night I was there with a date, two other couples and my mother. That wasn't odd at all, sometimes we'd fill up the entire place just with our

group. This night though it was just the seven of us. We took up a couple of tables, but since there were seven tables in the place five were empty.

Two couples walked in as we were being served. They were both very Mediterranean looking, both impeccably dressed. Carlo greeted them when they came in, as he did all of his guests.

"Welcome to Bomberas. How may I help you?" Carlo asked.

"We'd like to eat here this evening," the gentleman said.

"Do you have a reservation?" Carlo asked.

"No, sorry, we do not," the gentleman said.

"Then I'm sorry, but I cannot seat you. We are a reservations only restaurant," Carlo said. "If you will excuse me, I'm needed in the kitchen." Carlo turned and walked away.

The gentleman was obviously confused. He looked around and saw five empty tables. He had never been to Bomberas before or he would have known the policy. So I got up from the table and walked over to him.

"Excuse me," I said. "You want to eat here tonight?"

"Yea," he said. "We've heard that the food is fabulous."

"I'll tell you what. Let me show you how. There's a phone booth right outside the door. Go out there and call the restaurant. Make reservations for five minutes from now."

The man looked at me like I was a complete nut job. But I knew better. Since no one else but us were in there, I figured Carlo probably had enough food in the kitchen to feed these four, but he would not make an exception to his reservation only policy.

"You're kidding," the man said.

"Try it," I said.

All four of them walked out. I went back and sat down with my group. I told everybody what I told them. Now we were all curious to see what would happen next.

Sure enough, the phone rang. Carlo came out and picked it up. He asked the person on the phone how many people were coming and at what time. Carlo said, "Your table will be ready."

Walking back towards the kitchen, Carlo said, "Mary there will be four more dining tonight. They will be here in five to ten minutes."

Two minutes later the same four people walked in the door. Carlo went up to them, put his hands together like he never saw them before and said, "Welcome to Bomberas. How may I help you?"

"We'd like to eat here this evening," the gentleman said.

"Do you have a reservation?" Carlo asked.

"Yes, we do. We called you a few minutes ago," the gentleman said.

"Ah yes, your table is ready sir," Carlo said.

After they had been seated, the guy was shaking his head and smiling. He looked at me and we exchanged nods.

Forty five minutes later our meals were finished. After every meal at Bomberas, Carlo put a bottle of Anisette and another of Sambuca on the table along with glasses. Also, he put down a fresh pot of coffee. We all had a drink and it was time to go.

"Carlo," I said. "Can I have the check, please?"

Carlo came by and whispered in my ear. "Jimmy, that man over there at the table. He picked up your check. Your party's bill has been paid."

"What?" I said.

"Jim, he demanded it. I wasn't about to say no to this guy," Carlo said.

I got up and walked over to the table. Before I could say a word the gentleman said to me, "We're from New York City. My brother came here and ate a year ago. He came back and told me that the food here was better than what mama made at the restaurant.

"I'm only in town for one night and if it weren't for you I never would have been able to eat here. This is the best Italian food I've ever had. Thanks, young man."

We shook hands. I never knew exactly who this man was but if there is one thing I can spot, its money. This guy was super rich, I'd bet the farm on that. Also, it wouldn't surprise me at all to learn that he was one of the boys.

Six months later Mary told us a sad tale. Carlo was a flight instructor, small airplanes. He got in a bad plane wreck and I guess it disabled him so much that he was simply unable to keep working at the restaurant. He and Mary had done it together for many years, but now Mary told us that they had to close the doors.

That was a culinary tragedy. I never did hear what happened to Carlo and Mary Bombera, but I sure missed their food.

There was this group of Baccarat dealers at a big casino on the Strip. I knew who they were, but we were not close friends. Back in the day, large stake Baccarat games still used cash for betting in addition to checks. These boys got caught stuffing hundred dollar bills in their coat pockets when they opened up the game.

As far as I know, they did not receive any form of unofficial discipline from the boys. They did lose their Sherriff's cards which meant that they

could not work in any Nevada casino. Being enterprising men and decent amateur chefs they opened up a Mexican restaurant.

They called it "Banditos". The food was great and the name, what can I say. You get caught stealing from a joint and so you go open a restaurant called Banditos. How Vegas. How perfect.

Speaking of banditos…

The Villa D'Este was the place to go if you were one of the boys. Guys like Tony Spilotro (Joe Pesci's character in *Casino*) and his brother hung out there. It was a great restaurant. The people made it, but the whole scene was just really fantastic. This was the restaurant in the film *Casino* where Robert DeNiro, Sharon Stone and Joe Pesci all went to eat.

Well, I've never been an actor in a Hollywood film, but I used to go to the Villa D'Este. I'm sure (I don't know this for a fact, just my theory) that the FBI had to have some sort of permanent wire going at that place. The guy who was usually tending bar was a man named Cal Montana. He was Joe Montana's cousin, or so I was told.

I had a buddy who worked at the Trop by the name of Mike McKenna. Mike's brother was in the Nevada State Prison up in Carson City. Mike's brother caused some problems up there, so his name was in the paper a few times. I was in the Villa D'Este one night with Mike. It was about two thirty in the morning when we walked in. There was a couple of guys at the bar, a few others at the tables eating.

Cal was tending bar and he asked me what I wanted. I ordered a gin and tonic. Mike ordered a beer and he paid for my drink. Then Mike said, "Give those guys over there a drink on me too."

The guys across from us got their drinks and then one of the guys, he was short but very stocky, his hair was perfect, walked over to us and said, "Thanks for the drink."

"You're welcome," Mike said.

"I'm Tony Spilotro and this is my brother," Tony said.

We all shook hands. I introduced myself to the Spilotro brothers.

Tony sipped his drink and said, "You any relation to the McKenna whose doin' time up in Carson City?"

"Yep," Mike said, "that's my brother."

"Can you still work in the casinos? Given who your brother is?" Tony asked Mike.

"Yea, it's tough. I might have to change my name. Especially if I want to leave the Trop," Mike said.

"Whaddya gonna change it too?" Spilotro asked.

"I'm thinking about changing it to Spilotro," Mike said.

Tony started laughing and so did his brother. After a few minutes of laughing and back slapping, Tony said to the bartender, "You give these two sons a bitches anything they want. Don't let 'em pay for a thing."

Anthony "The Ant" Spilotro was not someone you ever wanted to cross. He was every bit as violent and unpredictable as Pesci's character in the film. This guy was a legend in Vegas. I have no personal knowledge of any of the bad things Tony Spilotro did, but I knew for sure that this guy was someone you simply needed to avoid.

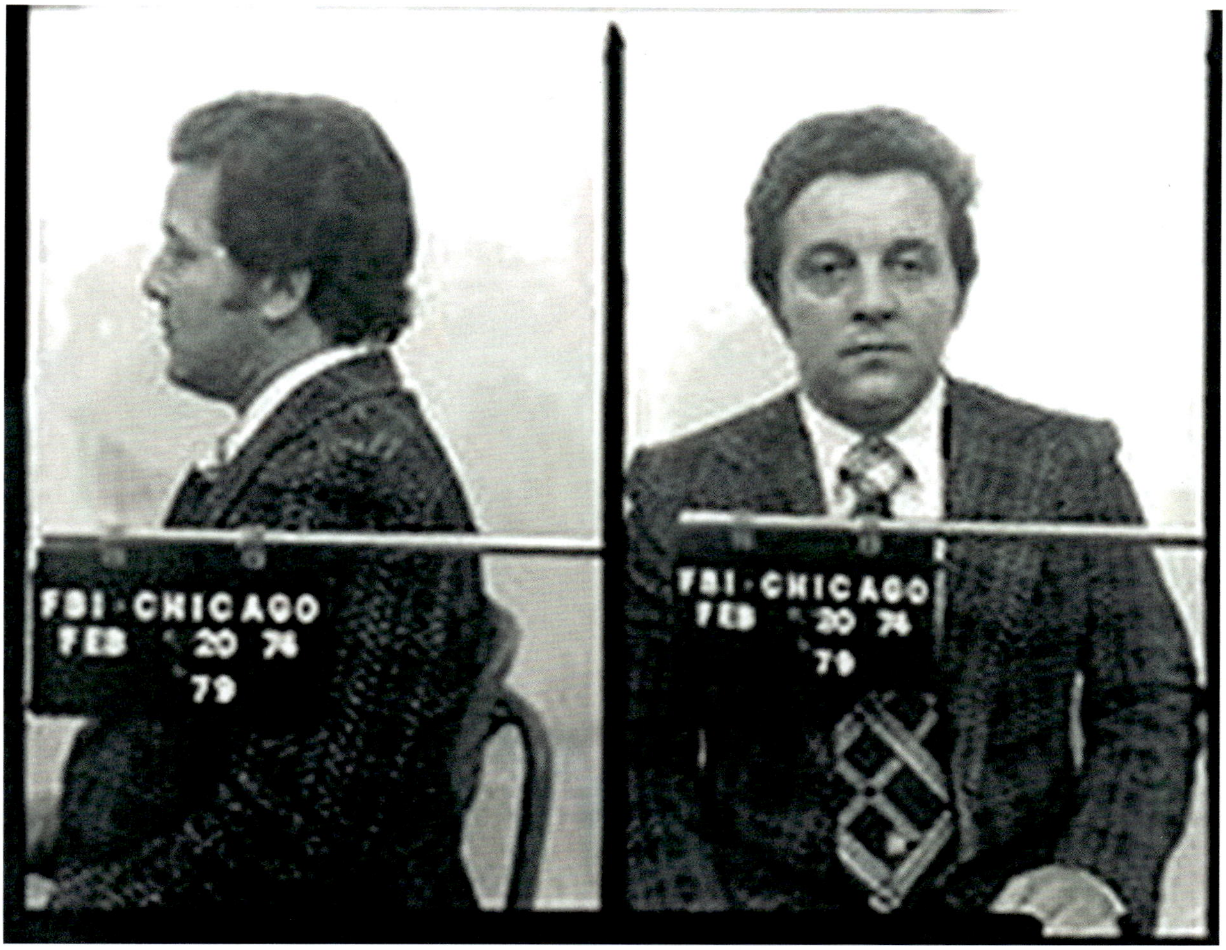

Tony Spilotro died a few years after I met him that night in the Villa D'Este. He was beaten to death in a field in Bensenville, Illinois and tossed into a shallow grave. That should tell you all you need to know.

About a year before this chance encounter in the Villa D'Este, Uncle Ed and I were talking one night. Ed told me that if I ever ran across Tony Spilotro to be very respectful, don't say anything bad and don't

do anything bad. In a nice, polite way, Ed went on, he told me to make up whatever excuse I needed to make and leave the man's presence as quickly as possible. Uncle Ed knew that Tony was nothing but trouble, a real loose cannon.

So after Tony offered to treat us to anything at the Villa D'Este I told Mike that I had to go pick up my girlfriend Linda and I left. I shook Tony's hand one more time and made sure that I ended the night on a good note.

I saw Tony Spiotro two or three more times at the Villa D'Este. Every time I saw him I bought him a drink and said hello, but I kept the whole encounter short and sweet. I always had an excuse ready to make a quick exit.

# A Sporting Life

I've always been an athlete. Basketball is my favorite sport. I played a bit in college and also in the Navy. Until Father Time took his toll on me, I played basketball recreationally on a regular basis.

Lehman's co-captains, Bob Delap and Jerry Looby.

*Row one:* Dave Bracken, Dave Phelps, Gary Deonise, Ralph Straub. *Row two:* Dick Weaver, Tom Hinkle, Jerry Looby, Jim Sinay, Dick Smith, Bob Delap, Bill Wentz.

**Jimmy's High School Basketball Team**

Back in the day, I went to the YMCA in downtown Vegas. We had some great pickup basketball games there every week. Every Wednesday afternoon a bunch of judges, lawyers and law enforcement guys played ball. They very graciously let me participate. Most of these men were older than me, but they could still hold their own.

One Wednesday a senior man in the Vegas branch of the FBI who was a regular participant in the pickup game took me aside. I'm not sure if he's still alive or not, so I'll use a made up name for him.

"Jimmy," Kevin said. "Can I speak to you for a minute?"

"Sure," I said, as I wiped my face with a towel. "What's up Kevin?"

Kevin motioned to me, indicating he wanted me to step to the side of the court so he could speak to me privately. "Jimmy, you've been seeing a lady, Alice, who lives on the west side of town."

I had not discussed my personal life with Kevin, ever. I was in fact seeing Alice, a beautiful lady who lived with a female roommate off of Charleston.

"Yea, I am," I said. "How did you know about -."

Kevin reached over, touched my arm and said, "Don't worry, Jimmy. I'm just looking out for you. One of our agents saw your car there and wrote down your plate number. Then he asked me if I knew you and I said I did."

Looking around, Kevin led me even farther away from a couple of lawyers who were standing ten feet from us and shooting the breeze. "That lady you're seeing, Alice. That's not her real name. Her name is Mary. Her husband is wanted by the FBI for murder and grand theft. We've been staking out her house for a while now. When he comes to see her, we're going to arrest him."

You coulda knocked me over with a feather. "She told me that she was divorced. I've never seen any evidence that another man is living there."

"He disappeared, but they are still married. Jimmy, you need to get the hell away from that lady. Her husband is a cold blooded killer. If he finds out that you've been seeing his wife, he'll kill ya."

Holy crap! I said to myself. I was more than a bit shaken. In my mind flashed the horrible image of some goon coming back in the middle of the night and putting a bullet in my head. My mother would be so ashamed of me, more for my stupidity than anything else.

"Kevin, I will never see Alice… Ah, Mary, ever again. You won't be seeing my car at her place or her car at mine. Thank you so much."

"Don't mention it, Jimmy. That's what friends are for."

On the way back to my apartment, I was thinking about just what I would tell Alice. Kevin made it clear to me that I could not let Alice know that I knew anything about her husband or her real identity.

Hmmm…. Hmmm… Then it came to me, the perfect plan.

"Hi baby," I said after I dialed Alice's number and she picked up the phone.

"Jimmy!" she said. "I can't wait to see you later. I'm making steaks for us."

"Alice," I said, trying to sound as serious as I could. "I just got back from the doctor's office. I've got a blood disease. It's rare and, honey, it's contagious."

"Contagious?!" Alice shrieked.

"Yea, I'm afraid so. Now we haven't been together for a week and the doctor told me that the odds of… you know… plus we've always used protection."

"Jimmy!"

Alice was wigging out and that's just what I wanted her to do. "You're okay, but I have to stop seeing you. In fact, I really can't see anybody for a while. I'm kinda like in a quarantine."

"A quarantine!"

"Now don't worry about me. I'll know more in a week. But until I tell ya honey, we just can't see each other. It's too risky for you."

We talked for another ten minutes and I tried my best to really sell it. I had to, it was literally a matter of life and death, just not in the way Alice knew.

I was very angry with her. Not telling me that she was still married was bad enough, but not to tell me that her psycho husband might pop in at any time and that oh, by the way, he was wanted for murder, well that was just plain mean.

A week later I called Alice back.

"Hi honey," I said.

"Jimmy, how are you?" Alice asked.

"Not good. I'm in for a long and involved treatment process. I'm afraid it's gonna take a miracle for me to be cured."

"Jimmy, are you… you gonna die?"

Not anytime soon since I'm out of your husband's line of fire, I thought but did not say. "It might come to that. But I'm a fighter, babe. I'm afraid though any type of dating is just out of the question for me. You are at zero risk of my disease. I double checked, not to worry."

"What's your disease called?" she asked.

"Ah… ah… It has some long Latin name. Dergontailus or Digitamitosis, something like that. Every time I hear the name it sends me into a depression. I try not to think about it."

I laid it on good and thick for the next ten minutes. Then I said goodbye and hung up.

Kevin told me a few weeks later that Alice, Mary, whatever her name was, just up and left one night. She disappeared, just like her old man. That coulda been me disappearing…

Next to basketball, golf is my favorite sport. The older I get the more I love golf because I can still play. There is just nothing better than a day at the golf course. Everything about it is fun, including the chance to meet new people.

More often than not I'd play at the Sahara Golf Course. About half the time I'd play as a single because a lot my golfing buddies had different days off than I did or worked different shifts. If the course was busy, which it often was, I could not play by myself so the course paired me up with someone. Almost every time this happened I met a nice guy or even a gal and we shared an afternoon on the links.

One day the starter asked me if I'd like a partner. It wasn't too busy so I was kinda surprised by the request. But hey, golf is a social game so I said sure. The starter said that my playing partner was waiting for me on the first tee, so I drove over in my cart and saw an older African American gentleman waiting for me.

I got out of the cart, walked over to him, stuck out my hand and said, "Jim Sinay."

"Herb Mills," the man said.

It took me a minute, but then it hit me. Herb Mills? The Mills Brothers?

"The Mills Brothers?" I asked.

"Yea," Herb said.

I told Herb that when I was a kid I used to watch him and his brothers perform on TV. I had a few Mills Brothers 45s when I was a kid too. The Mills Brothers were a big deal, although probably not too many people alive today could tell you about them. Back in the 1930s they were the first African Americans to have their own network radio show. They performed with the best of their time – Bing Crosby, Cab Calloway, Ella Fitzgerald, Duke Ellington and Tommy Dorsey. They had number one hit songs through the 1950s. I was playing golf with a living legend.

"I saw you guys perform at the Casablanca in Canton, Ohio," I told Herb.

"That's true," Herb said. "Boy was that a long time ago. Canton was a really nice town. We loved playing there."

Golfing with him was an absolute pleasure. We talked about Vegas and music and the decade I grew up, the 1950s. He could not have been a more polite and wonderful gentleman.

This one bar we used to go to once in a while, The Philly Pub, had an annual golf outing over in Pahrump. If you've lived in or visited Vegas, then you probably know that prostitution is illegal in Clark County, where Vegas is. Now when I say it's illegal, let's keep it real. Especially back in the day, the cops did not bust people for prostitution unless something else was going on to, like drug dealing or theft, etc. None of the powers at be in Vegas back then (or now I assume), wanted men to come to Vegas and have to worry about getting busted for purchasing the services of a prostitute.

What the civic leaders of Clark County did not want then and surely do not want now were cat houses springing up on every corner. So just north of Vegas, a forty five minute drive right over the mountain, Pahrump legalized prostitution and the cat houses sprang up there.

Anywho… The Philly Pub had this golf tournament out in Pahrump and a party at the cat house later. They gave away prizes for the longest drive, closest to the pin, etc. – the usual golf tournament stuff. Only the prizes were not a sleeve of golf balls or drinks at the bar - the prizes were sex at the cat house.

I went to this tournament one year with a friend of mine named Bill Fesi. We got paired up with two guys who were from out of state. On the

first tee, one of these out of state guys walks over and gives me a small, glass vial.

"What's this?" I asked.

"Some stuff to make ya happy," the man said. Then he walked back to his golf cart.

I looked at Bill and asked, "Is this coke?"

"It looks like it, Jimmy," Bill said.

"I've never done coke," I said.

"Neither have I, Jimmy. I know plenty of people who have."

In the 1980s, cocaine use was common in Vegas. I was the exception and not the rule by abstaining from it. I drank plenty, but I just didn't indulge in illegal drugs. Back then, there was no such thing as employment drug testing, so if you were a dealer and you wanted to snort coke no one would stop you.

As you might guess by now, I'm apt to try anything once. The time seemed right, setting seemed right, so I said to Bill, "Wanna try some?"

"Why not," Bill said.

So we put some coke on our palms and sniffed it up our nose. Bill looked at me and me at him and we started giggling. As the day went on, every couple of holes or so, Bill and I would stop and sniff this stuff. I wasn't crazy about it, but I was feeling no pain by the eighteenth hole.

One of our playing partners said, "We need to hit a ball over those trees. That means hitting the ball over 300 yards. Otherwise, there is no way we are going to get on in two. We're playing pretty good; if we eagle this hole, who knows? We might win."

It was a best ball tournament. All of the players in my group had used up their drives, so they had to use my drive on this hole. That wasn't the good news.

I got up to the ball and looked at Bill. He started laughing and so did I. Rather than worry about it, I just let it fly. I crushed it. The ball flew over the trees. We got it up and down and eagled the hole. Because my drive was the longest one of the day, I won a free session with a hooker.

**Jimmy and Bill Fesi**

So a while later we went to the cathouse. I went into the room with the nice lady, I got naked and so did she. I was laughing the whole time. I kept waiting for something to happen, for my anatomy to respond, but it was no use. Cocaine was definitely not an aphrodisiac for me. Rather than waste the gift, I turned my free pass over to one of the guys who was sober enough to make good use of it.

That was the one and only time I ever did cocaine. While it made me laugh, I just didn't like the overall feeling. Plus I'd seen too many people get strung out on the stuff to the point where it controlled their lives.

I only had one other personal experience with narcotics…

My roommate Don had to get his paycheck cashed at this bar on West Spring Mountain Road. I drove him out there in my Cadillac Eldorado. It was mid-afternoon. When we got there, we sat down and ordered coffee.

One of the patrons at the bar said to us, "Hey, there's a birthday party tonight for Gordo. Wanna piece of cake?"

I said, "I'll take a small piece."

This lady, who neither Don nor I had ever seen before, cut out two small pieces of cake and set them down in front of us.

"You can have mine, Jimmy," Don said. "I'm not in the mood for cake right now."

So I ate a couple of slices of chocolate cake. We finished our coffee, Don cashed his check. We went outside and jumped in the caddy and headed home.

Driving down Spring Mountain Road back towards the Strip, I got this funny feeling. Something was definitely not right with me.

I was squirming. It felt there were a million little ants crawling all over me.

"Don, somethin's wrong," I said.

"What?" Don said.

"My body feels weird. My head is swimming. I mean it, I'm not doin' good at all," I said.

At the next stop light, I got out of the car and switched places with Don. He drove the rest of the way home.

"You're white as a sheet," Don said to me.

I felt like someone had given me death. I felt cold inside. Like I was going crazy or something, losing my mind.

I was supposed to go to work that night at six o'clock. I jumped in the shower. That didn't do me any good, I still felt terrible. So I took three more showers. No improvement.

It was pretty obvious what happened. Don got on the phone and called up to the bar and said, "What the hell was in that cake?" Don listened to what the person on the other end of the line was saying and then said, "You're kidding me." Then Don hung up.

"Well?" I said, still as jumpy as a frog on a hotplate.

"Jim, there was PCP in that damn cake."

"What do I do?" I said. "I can't function! I'm supposed to go to work tonight."

Don told me to eat some bread and butter. I did. I wasn't hungry anymore, but my craziness was still raging. Then Don made another phone call. He called a lady friend of his. She told Don that she'd bring a pill over for me.

The nice woman brought a pill over for me. I took it and felt a little better. It was a downer of some kind I assume, something to calm me down. I drove to work and went to see my boss.

"Jim, you're white as a sheet. What's wrong?" my boss said.

I told him the whole story. He knew that I didn't do drugs and the story was too weird to make up.

"Head on home, Jim," my boss said. "I'll have someone cover for ya. Stay away from any more cake!"

"Very funny," I said and thanked my lucky stars that I had a very nice and understanding boss.

I went home and called my girlfriend. She brought over some medication which calmed me down. I went to bed and slept for 14 hours. I got up the next day and I was still exhausted, but I made it through and life went on.

A few days later we heard that two people overdosed on PCP at that "birthday party" and went to the hospital. The police were investigating what the hell went on. I would never take PCP on purpose! It's like swallowing an insanity pill. It's beyond me how anyone could take that stuff thinking he was gonna have a good time.

# The Tropicana

In the 1980s, some of the biggest dice games in Vegas were played at the Tropicana Hotel. I wanted in on that action. There would always be time to "put the coat back on" – to be a pit boss or a floor supervisor, a casino executive. So I made the decision to leave the Silverbird and deal craps again at the Trop.

Some people though, when they put the coat on, became instant assholes…

On my first night dealing craps at the Trop, I started on the stick. I really liked the three people I was working with and we were having a good time. The dice got hot. Every time they won I shouted out with enthusiasm, "Winner eight" or "Winner nine." We were all having fun and that's what it's all about.

There was this pit boss. He was a white guy in his forties and bald. He was constantly chomping on a cigar. I'd never seen him before that night and he'd never seen me. Every time I called out "Winner!" his face got red. Obviously, he didn't like my style.

After my shift had ended, I took all the tokes we made, several hundred dollars, and brought them over to the box we used to hold them (each table had its own box for tokes). As I was putting the tokes in the box, this little bulldog of a pit boss came over to me and got his face right up in mine and said,

"Do you always call the goddamn dice that way?"

I took a step back and said, "I only call the top of the dice sir. Nothing else."

He grumbled something or another and went on his way. He never bothered me after that night because I think he found out I just took the coat off and I could give less than a shit about him.

A lot of guys just couldn't handle wearing the coat. A little bit of power goes to some people's heads. Nobody liked this guy and maybe that's the way he wanted it. But despite jerks like that guy, this story should tell you all you need to know as to why I wanted to deal dice at the Tropicana…

A man came in one night to play craps. I didn't know his name, but we were told that he was a big time securities executive from New York City, a Wall Street guy. We opened a game up for him at nine o'clock. We raised the limits on the game for him. The high roller table at the Trop, the game I worked in, normally had $5000 bets with $10,000 odds, the money you could put behind your bet on the pass line. For this guy, the house raised the limits to $15,000 bets and $30,000 odds. His credit line was one million dollars.

The man stood on my end of the table and asked for $100,000 in checks. I cut him out $100,000 in $5000 checks. He put $10,000 on the line with $20,000 odds. He kept rolling and placed $10,000 and $20,000 bets on the numbers five, nine and ten. The next roll of the dice was seven out. I locked up all the checks. Eighty thousand dollars. The guy lost eighty grand in less than two minutes.

"Give me another $100,000," the man asked me.

"Yes sir," I said.

It went on like this for eight hours. At the end of our eight hour shift this Wall Street man was down $1.2 million dollars. It was five a.m. Another crew took over for us. I went home and went to bed. I got up the next day and went back to work that night.

The same guy was still playing at the same table.

I talked to one of the bosses who was standing to the side.

"What the hell?" I said. "How's he doin'?"

"This guy was out $1.6 million dollars. Then all of a sudden he caught fire. He went from $1.6 million loser to $1.3 million winner. Right now, he's up about $600,000."

We went to work on another table. The guy stayed until 6 a.m. in the morning. When he was through playing, he had lost $2 million dollars.

The casino boss said to the man, "Go home sir, back to New York. Write us a check for $1.5 million. I'll write off the $500,000 if you agree to come back in two weeks and play some more. I'll give you another $1 million dollar credit line when you come back."

The guy signed the deal and said okay. The casino paid for the air fare, the room (penthouse suite), food and everything else.

Two weeks later the man came back. He had a $1 million dollar credit line. He played for 20 hours and ended up losing $1.75 million bucks.

Going up to the boss the man said, "How much are you gonna write off this time?"

The boss said, "Nothin'. Write us a check for $1.75 million."

The guy scowled a bit, then he wrote the check. The casino called the bank to make sure it would clear and it did. We saw the guy at the casino the next day. He didn't gamble at all – he saw a show, had dinner, etc. He got on the plane and went back home.

The Trop cleaned up. On the man's first trip, the house won $1.5 million. The $500,000 they used for a write off, which reduced the casino's tax bill. Then the guy dropped $1.75 million more. The Trop took in over $3 million bucks from this one bettor.

This man should have quit when he was up a million plus. Also, he didn't have to come back. The house knew just how to handle him and boy did they handle him. What's the old saying? A fool and his money are soon parted.

I've seen this same scenario play out a million times. Yea, I've watched people make some dough at the tables. I always smile when winners leave with their pockets full because that's not normally what happens.

We did have some good times at the Trop. We made a lot of money and we shared some laughs. One night I went to work with a crew of three short guys. They had a nickname, "The Munchkins". Boy could those guys deal a craps game! They hustled bets like nobody's business and everyone at their game left with a smile whether they won or lost. They were some really funny fellas.

I'm 6'4" tall. So when we went to work that night we were quite the sight. Me towering over the three Munchkins. Everybody got a good laugh out of that. The Munchkins started doing their thing and soon enough the dice pit was rockin'.

A group of guys from Texas showed up. They had on cowboy hats and they were all talkin' in that famous Texas drawl. They loved me and the Munchkins and the dice got hot. The Munchkins kept saying, "Put a hundred on the pass line for dealers" and "How 'bout a hardway eight for the little people?" On my end of the table, I had as many as five or six

**Fred Orme, One Of The Munchkins**

bets for me on the pass line and on the numbers. Those Texas fellas were making points and rollin' numbers. I was raking in $200, $300, $500 in winnings just for the dealers every time those guys roiled the dice. This went on for an hour, then another hour, then another…

There is a box in the pit desk where all the dealer tokes go. That's where the Munchkins and I were putting all those checks we were rakin' in. In one shift, that dealer's toke box got filled up ten times. When the box got filled, a dealer would take the tokes to the cage and exchange them for cash. Then the dealer put the cash in his pocket holding it for everyone to split when the shift was over.

After this incredible shift ended the Munchkins and I were all fired up. Not only did we have a blast, but we knew that the night's tokes were gonna be awesome. We all sat down in a room in the back and counted out the dough. None of us had ever seen anything like this before from a regular (not high roller) crap game. We had $45,000 sitting in front of us.

Each Munchkin got $10,000 and I took $10,000. We decided to split the $5000 left with all our bosses. Needless to say, we made our bosses very happy.

It's just one of those nights you never forget. The chemistry was right. The dice were red hot. Whatever stars had to align just aligned. What a great memory.

There was another bad pit boss at the Trop that I remember well. Like the bald guy I ran into when I first started working at the Trop, Tom (names changed to protect the guilty) was a wimpy little popcorn fart of a dude who thought he was somebody because he had the coat on. For weeks he'd been out to get me, although I didn't really know why.

He didn't like me, for whatever reason – maybe because I was tall and popular with the ladies.

I opened a craps game one night and I noticed that Tom was scrutinizing my every move. That didn't really bother me because I did my job the right way no matter who was watching. After my shift at the table was over, I cleaned my hands and went to take my break. Tom intercepted me, handed me a piece of paper and said, "This is for you."

It was a warning slip. In a casino, a dealer is given a warning slip if he's doing something he should not be doing but it's not a serious enough offense to merit immediate termination. If you got three warning slips, you lost your job.

"What's this for?" I asked.

"Handling checks wrong," Tom said.

What Tom didn't know is that I'd already been warned by a buddy of mine that Tom was gonna give me a warning slip that night – not for any particular reason other than to just screw with me. I tore the warning slip in two and put it in his coat pocket. Then I looked Tom in the eye and said, "You can stick your warning slip up your ass. I already heard you were gonna give me a warning slip for nothin'. How would you like the bosses to hear about this shit? Don't ever try this crap with me again or you won't like what happens."

Tom looked at me, turned around and started watching another craps game.

After this incident, Tom and I never got along. We kept a respectable distance from each other. Then one night Tom was the floor boss. His buddy was the pit boss. They started to give me and my craps dealing

crew a hard time for no reason at all. It made what should have been a very pleasant night an ordeal.

Around three a.m. or so that morning, after work, I walked into a little bar just down the street from the Trop. Tom and his pit boss buddy were sitting at the bar. We'd made a good score that night and when dealers made a bunch of money in tokes, they shared some of it with the floorman and the pit boss. So I approached them to give them some dough.

I said to Tom, "This money is from the other three guys on the crew, not me." Then I threw the pit boss some money and told him the same thing.

"We can go outside if you guys don't like it," I said. "One at a time or both at once, your choice." I was pissed and I'd had enough.

Those two cowards wouldn't even look at me. I hate spineless jerks. If you wanna give someone shit, at least be man enough to back it up. Not these two, they were gutless. So I said, "Don't ever give me a warning slip again. I know how to do my job. You two little weasels can kiss my ass."

I finished my drink, paid my tab and walked out.

I never heard a word from either of those guys during the last two years I worked at the Tropicana.

One night I came into work as usual and I noticed this tall guy, about my height 6'4" or so, in a suit and glasses standing in the pit. He was real thin and his skin was grey, like people's skin gets when their sick. I thought he looked familiar, but I couldn't place him. So I asked the boss who he was.

"That's Rock Hudson, Jimmy," my boss said.

Damned if it wasn't, but it sure didn't look like him. He was battling AIDS, but I don't recall anyone really knowing that back then or even what AIDS was all about.

"You're kidding," I said.

"Nope, their making a movie called *The Vegas Strip Wars*. It's a TV movie I think."

"Wow. Man, he doesn't look like the Rock Hudson I've seen in the movies," I said. Then I went about the business of dealing craps.

Later that night Pat Morita came walking into the pit. I was dealing the game on table one. Rock Hudson came up behind him. Then a guy with lights and a camera appeared. They were filming the movie! The boss told me to keep my eyes on the game and act normal, so I did.

When the film came out I was curious to see if I was in it. Sure enough, there I was. Me and my friend Moon Mullins and Johnny Dipetta. The

movie was okay I guess, but I love it because it's kind of a time capsule. This was Vegas just before the mega-corps, the Steve Wynns and that crowd, changed the place forever.

For some reason after my film debut Hollywood didn't come calling. Never quite understood why not …

# Cheaters

For as long as there's been gambling, there have been cheaters. Sorta like ham and eggs, they just go together.

As I've said, the boys didn't tolerate cheaters. They dealt with them swiftly and surely. The way they caught most of the cheats was by watching the games from above. Around 1980 or so most of the big joints had cameras installed; "the eye in the sky" which recorded all of the action on video tape. But before 1980 there were men in the room above the game looking down at the tables with binoculars. If they saw something fishy, they'd use a radio or phone to call down to the casino floor and alert the supervisors.

I was working one night downtown when a buddy of mine told me what happened during the previous shift. No one had heard from the guy in the room above the game for a couple of hours. Usually the man watching the action reported in every so often. So a couple of the bosses went up there to see what was going on.

They found Mr. Eagle Eye standing up on the side of the room. He had his headphones on and a cassette tape playing on his portable tape player. He was also smoking a joint. Needless to say, the boys were not amused. For all they knew he could have been deliberately not doing his job to let his buddies rob the house blind. At worse he was a lazy bum.

They found that guy a few hours later out back with a couple of broken bones lying unconscious by the trash cans. He'd probably tell ya that wasn't worth it to cross the boys, it never was…

Years later when I became the boss I saw some interesting things. I remember one night down at the Boulder Station. I was on my break eating dinner when I was paged. The guys in the dice pit wanted me to take a look at a game. They couldn't figure out what was going on, but they knew the action wasn't right. Okay, I told 'em, give me a minute to finish eating and I'll be right there.

"What's up?" I said as I walked into the security room.

"We're not sure Jimmy. Take a look at this," a security guy said as he switched on the tape.

I watched the shooter carefully at full speed. His movements seemed a little stilted, but I didn't see anything wrong at first. Then I slowed it down. When I watched it frame by frame, I saw what was going on. The shooter was throwing one die and slipping the other one in his buddy's boot. This guy was super slick. When he threw the one die across the table, his partner would reach out and place a late bet, something that was against the rules but not always enforced, and drop a second die with a six showing on top. They had it timed perfectly. Unless you were really looking for it, the move was very hard to see.

What these cheaters were doing was making sure that a number rolled greater than seven. They had field and number bets all over the table. They made a few grand in half an hour using this scheme. After that night, they never did it again. No, there were no more "boys" to turn them over to by this time (it was in the 1990s), but they were tossed out and blacklisted.

It is illegal to count cards in the State of Nevada. But let me be specific about what it means to "count cards". If you're smart enough to remember every card that's been dealt in your head then Vegas is all yours, baby. There is no rule or law that regulates a person's memory. Remember the movie *Rainman* with Tom Cruise and Dustin Hoffman? Hoffman's character, an autistic guy with the rare genius of being able to count cards or anything else, made Cruise's character a ton of money playing blackjack. I've personally never seen anyone do that, successfully count a six deck card shoe, but no doubt some people are better at counting cards than others.

Most people have to cheat to count cards. By cheat I mean using any form of artificial/mechanical device to count cards – a clicker, a computer, a camera, anything other than the brain and the brain alone. At a 21 table, the only cards that need to be counted are the tens, jacks, queens, kings and the two, three, four, five and six. The idea is that when the cards are in your favor, you bet more. When the cards are not, you bet less or fold.

I was working at the Dunes one day in the late 1980s. I was supervising the 21 pit. There was a player on "third base", which is the first spot on the right of the dealer ("first base" being the first spot on his left), who was sitting in a wheelchair. The dealer accidently tossed a card to the floor. The dealer cannot pick up a card that's been tossed on the floor, they aren't allowed to take their eyes off of the layout.

"Jim, card on the floor," the dealer called out to me.

"Okay, no problem," I said. When I bent over to pick the card up, I noticed the man in the wheelchair was tapping the right side of his wheelchair, where his foot rested. I wondered, why would he be doing that? A nervous tick or something?

As a supervisor, I was paid to be suspicious. So I stood back away from the man and watched him more closely. His left hand was opening and closing in a rhythmic way as was his right hand and he was tapping both hands on the end his armrest.

Hmmm… Hmmm…

I called the eye in the sky and said, "On BJ 23 (Blackjack table 23). There's a guy in the wheelchair. Get a good close view of what's goin' on with his feet and his armrest." The eye in the sky was on it, so I went to watch another game.

Ten minutes later the phone rang. It was the eye in the sky. "Sir," the man said to me, "this guy is using a counter."

"What kind?" I asked.

"He's keeping track of the ten, jack, queen and kings with his left foot and it's registering on the edge of his armrest. The two, three, four, five and six he's keeping track of with his right foot. The results are posted on his right hand armrest. He's resetting his counter zero with his thumbs when the dealer re-shuffles."

"Okay, got it." I called security and I told them I need three guards. They came down to the pit.

"See the gentleman in the wheelchair?" I told the guards.

"Yes sir," they said.

"Take him away, book him and call Metro. Get his picture, ID, fingerprints, the whole thing. He's using a mechanical device to count cards."

"The guy in the wheelchair?" one of the guards asked. He wanted to be double sure before he arrested a disabled man.

"Yep, that guy," I said, pointing.

So the guards went over to the table and addressed the guy in the wheelchair. "Sir," one of the guards said, "Take your checks please and come with us."

"Whaadya talkin' about?" the guy in the wheelchair said.

"Please come with us," the guards said.

As the guards where wheeling the guy away, he started screaming and hollering. "Where in the hell are you taking me? Why are you hassling me?"

The people at the table were looking at me like I was the meanest bastard ever to walk the face of the earth. I could not say a word about what I knew because if I did then I could get dragged into court and have to testify about what I said, what everyone else said, etc., etc. So I just offered, "It was something that had to be done."

When I walked away from that game, I got booed. Those people gave me the Bronx cheer because all they knew is that mean old Jim the Supervisor took this poor, old disabled guy away from the blackjack game. That's the only time in my life I've ever been booed.

Vegas was fun back in the early 70s. It was definitely a wide open type town. It was a small enough place though that if you screwed up, if you were a thief or a slacker, your name was mud pretty damn quickly. There was sort of an unofficial system of justice if you will. It worked great too and it was largely fair. Hey, it wasn't perfect, but then what is?

Each casino handled stealing differently. It's been years, I know, but I still prefer not to name names. I recall a couple of incidents at the joints. One place downtown… Anyway you did not want to get caught stealing there. A dealer we knew was sticking checks in his waistband. Well, security grabbed him and they took him downstairs for "questioning".

Along the way, he made a helluva mess. There were bloodstains from where his head hit the wall on the way to the holding cell. It seems as if he just couldn't keep his balance walking down those stairs…

Same casino, different guy. This thief they found in the bushes out back. Both his hands were broken. He must have fallen down or something. Strange how these accidents happened to the same types of people at the same casino…

Stealing and cheating were just very bad ideas. If you had any brains at all you simply avoided those pursuits.

The boys didn't mind losing once in a while. But back in the day, if they started losing too much at a 21 table they called in a mechanic. A mechanic in card terms is someone who can deal you whatever cards he desires from a deck. Yea, that's cheatin'. Yea, back in the day if someone was takin' too much of the house's dough, they called in a mechanic.

These mechanics were not well known to other casino employees. In fact, their very existence was a secret, but an open one. I watched one in action one night. Some guy was winning big on the blackjack table. Then the mechanic stepped in. Suddenly the cards went the other way. Wisely, the guy quit playing when the tide turned against him.

Nowadays if a casino got caught employing a mechanic someone would be going to jail. Back in the 70s the boys used mechanics to limit their losses and no one said a word about it. It's just the way it was.

# Heading for the Exit

When the twenty first century dawned, a number of things were happening in my life that all pointed in the same direction. My days of working in Vegas were drawing to a close. The Vegas I knew and loved had died a decade plus earlier. Everything was corporate now. The boys were long gone forced out by a bigger outfit, Wall Street.

But I really did love my job and that kept me going for a while. When a new resort opened on the Strip, I went to work there as a Floor Supervisor. Seemed like a good move in terms of money and work environment.

I was right about the money, but boy was I wrong about the workplace.

It wasn't long after I started at this mega-resort when I began to clash with the new crowd. As a Supervisor, I was a stickler for certain things. Having dealt and supervised games for three decades, I think I'd learned a thing or two. That's why I was hired, or so I thought.

Four ladies were dealing a crap game one night. I was watching the action and doing my job. A bunch of guys were surrounding this table and making all sorts of bets for the women dealers. That's great I said, that's Vegas. Good for them.

Problem was the bets being made for the dealers were not being handled properly. In Nevada, making a bet for the dealers is allowed, but if the bet is a winner the dealers cannot let the bet "ride", keep it on the

table and live, unless the bettor says it's okay to do so. All the bettor has to say is "Leave the bet for the dealers" and it stays.

The ladies dealing this game were benefiting from a hot dice roll. The guys were making $50 bets for themselves and $25 bets for the dealers on the pass line. However, when the pass line was a winner the dealers were not removing the bets and guys playing were not telling them that the bets should ride.

Addressing the stick person I said, "Please remove those bets for the dealers and put the money in the center."

Rather than getting a "Yes sir" I got an earful from the lady on the stick.

"Why? What's the problem?" she said.

"The bettor has to say 'Let it ride' or the money comes off the line. That's the rule in Nevada."

"Well," she said, "that's not how it is in Atlantic City."

This lady dealer was arguing with me, in front of customers! I was floored and really ticked off. "Take the money off the pass line. If you refuse to do that you're off this game right now."

I got a dirty look from all the lady dealers, but the stick person finally did as she was told. I walked away thinking, what the hell is wrong with these people? You don't question a supervisor during a live game. Who trained them?

A couple of hours later I got called upstairs to a Casino Executive's office.

"Sinay, leave those girls alone, the ones dealing craps," he said to me.

"Sir," I said and proceeded to tell him exactly what happened.

To my total shock and amazement this executive said to me, "I don't give a damn what you think, Sinay. I said leave those girls alone. What part of 'leave those girls alone' do you not understand?"

I got it. The exec didn't care if the dealers broke the rules and the law. Okay, I said. This is not the industry I worked in for thirty years. These are not the people I used to know and respect.

The writing was on the wall. I was either gonna get fired or I would quit.

The very next day after this happened I went to work and opened a crap game. I removed the lid and moved it a few inches so I could count the checks. Sitting on top of the checks was piece of paper called a closing slip. It gives the person who sealed the game's closing count – how much money is there in the form of checks. I had to be sure the closing slip total matched the total checks I counted when I reopened the game. If there was a discrepancy between the closing slip and my count, I had to report it.

While I'm counting out the checks, the girl on the stick who was waiting for me to finish said to me, "Jim, what do you think of girls working in the dice pit?"

I said, just making casual conversation, "I've known a couple of ladies who had some problems when they got pregnant because they couldn't bend over easily to take care of the table."

She said, "My husband would agree with you on that."

We chit chatted for a second and I finished counting. I turned around to hand the slip to the pit clerk and the stick lady at the table shouted out as loud as she could, "Why do I have to work with a man who does not want women in the dice pit?"

Funny thing, standing out in front of the game was the casino executive I'd had the meeting with the night before. He had two security guards by his side. They took me into the office, I turned in my card for that casino and walked out.

That wasn't my last job in Vegas. I got another job at another place within a day. Still though I could see it comin'. There was no place for me in Vegas anymore. I was a dinosaur.

Months later I heard that the whole crowd, the casino executive and the Atlantic City lady craps dealers, were all fired when higher ups caught them doing things the wrong way. I wished it had been me who caught 'em, but I was long gone.

♠♦♣♥ ♥♣♦♠

I knew that I'd had enough. It just wasn't fun anymore. The boys were gone. The town was run by business executives. I wasn't Jim Sinay anymore to the bosses, I was just a number. My little Vegas now had 2 million people in it. Most of my friends were gone – retired, dead or simply moved on. Crime was bad and getting worse. I was just too damned old to deal with the new Vegas and all its nonsense.

As it goes with many things in life, everything started to move in the same direction. In November of 1999 my Aunt Delores told Mom that she was very ill. Mom had promised her parents that when her sister needed her, she'd be there for her. Mom and I talked about this over at my house.

"I've got 32 years in the business, Mom," I said. "Let's go back to Ohio. I'll give them notice at work and we'll go back to Ohio."

**Jimmy And His Mom**

So, In March of 2000 I put my house up for sale. It sold in a flash because Vegas was going through a real estate boom. By the middle of April, we were on our way back to Ohio. Mom flew. She wanted to spend some time with her old friend Jane Stoffer. I loaded up the moving van, got my car in tip top shape and I drove. I wanted to take my time heading back and see some old friends along the way.

At first Mom and I rented a place, but we didn't completely get settled. We wanted to buy a house. Pretty soon we found a condo that we really liked so we moved there. I thought everything was going to go along smoothly for a while, but that's not usually how life goes with me…

My aunt's health deteriorated rapidly. We had to sell her house and property and put her in a nursing home. Then Mom got colon cancer. She struggled with that and had to be put in a nursing home too. That just about broke my heart.

One day Mom said to me, "Jimmy, can you take me home please? I'd like to die in my own bed."

So that's exactly what I did. I bought her a nice, queen sized adjustable bed (like a hospital bed). I bought her a huge brand new TV. We got her a bird feeder too so she could watch the birds through the sliding glass window. A nurse or an aide came by for an hour a day to give Mom a bath, change her sheets and change her ostomy bags.

I picked up mom and put her in the wheelchair from time to time and wheeled her through the neighborhood. She loved doing that when the weather was nice. Mom's friend Janice spent a lot of time with her too. Then Jane Stoffer died. Gradually Mom's health got worse. After a couple of years at home, she couldn't move around much or do anything.

One day Mom said to me, "This is no way to live, Jimmy. I wish God would take me."

"Mom," I said. "If I could pick any woman in the world to be my mom, including the Queen of England, it would be you."

Mom smiled and looked at me and said, "Really?"

"Really, Kid," I said.

"You're the kid, remember?" she said.

"I know Mom. I love ya."

We held hands and cried for a while. I thank God that Mom was with me through this difficult time. It was the least I could do given everything she'd done for me over the years. Mom always found something to laugh about, even when she was so sick she could barely talk. What an inspiration she was to me and all of her friends.

Not long after that we had to admit Mom to the hospital. Her blood pressure was 50 over 25. The doctor said to me, "Mr. Sinay, your mom won't be leaving this hospital." He told me to go home and get some rest. He said someone would call me when it was time.

The phone rang two hours later. I hurried back to the hospital. Mom was sleeping when I got there. I grabbed her hand and I started talking to her. I didn't know if she could hear me or not. I thanked her for everything.

Dad had died in 1995. Mom joined him on January 25th, 2005.

My best friend was gone, my buddy, my mother. The only family I had left was my brother Bob out in Vegas.

We had a funeral Mass for Mom at Central Catholic Church. Per her request, I read this letter aloud at her Mass. It was her message to everyone from Heaven:

"To my dearest friends and family. There are some things I'd like to say, but first of all you should know that I have arrived okay. I'm writing this from heaven where I do all with God above. There is no more tears or sadness, just His eternal love. Please don't be unhappy just because I'm out of sight, because I am still with you every morning, noon and night. The day I had to leave you when my life on earth was through, God picked me and hugged me and said 'I welcome you'. He made a list

of many things He wants me now to do and foremost on His special list is watching over all of you.

"When you think of our life on earth and all our loving years, because you're only human it is bound to bring you tears. Do not be afraid to cry, it does relieve the pain, remember that there are no flowers unless we have the rain. I sure wish I could tell you all what God has planned, but even if I did you wouldn't understand. One thing is for certain though I live on Earth no more, but I'm closer to you now than I ever was before.

"There are many rocky roads ahead and many hills to climb, but together we will do it one day at a time. It was always my philosophy and I'd like it for you too, that as you give unto the world the world will give to you. So if you meet someone who is feeling sad and low, lend a hand to pick him up as on your way you go. When you walk down the street and have me on your mind, I'll be right there in your footsteps only half a step behind. When it's time for you to go from that body to be free, remember you're not going you're coming here to me."

I cried when I read this letter at Mom's Mass. Twice I had to stop and take a moment. Mom was everything to me.

It was snowing at the graveside when we laid my mother to rest. I remember Mom telling me that it was snowing like crazy the day she was born in 1917. Standing there watching them prepare the grave I had this feeling, a knowingness, that the snow was sending me a message from my mother. It was her way of saying to me, "Jimmy, you Big Dummy, I'm alright. Don't worry about me."

Ever since that day my world has been dimmer. A light went out for me. I know that one day I'll see Mom again and I know that's she's in Heaven, but I guess I feel bad for myself because I'm stuck on Earth for a while without her.

Do I have regrets? Sure. I absolutely love kids, always have, but I have none of my own. I'm not married so there is no wife to comfort me as I grow older. Things could have been so different. I could have stayed in Ohio, gone back to college, taught school, got married, had eight kids and lived that life. But I didn't. I went to Vegas.

The truth is I would not trade my life for anyone else's. I wish (and hope now through this book) that I could reconnect with some of my old

friends, male and female. I've lost touch with most of them and many of them have passed on.

What my friends and I shared back in the day was a time and place that was truly unique in American history. It just doesn't work to look back on Vegas in the 70s and 80s through the eyes of 2015 and make judgments about people and events. I think the best way to consider those times is to take them for what they were and smile. There will never be another Frank Sinatra or Elvis Presley or Harry Claiborne or Teddy Binion. Those men were a product of their times and those times are long gone.

My memory bank is full. Whenever I want to relive the past I just close my eyes and walk back into the Sahara in 1975 or the Trop in 1980. I live a quiet life now in Ohio. I love my dear friends here every bit as much as I loved everyone out in Vegas.

If I could pass on any wisdom to the younger generation it would be this – if you have a dream, go for it. You only live once and time flies by so fast. What you will regret most in life are not things you've done, but the things you didn't do because you were afraid to try. Life is a game, play it well. Don't let the loser seven rolls get ya down, you'll roll a winner next time. Keep your vices in check and keep your heart open.

Next time you're out at the bar with your pals, lift a toast to us old Vegas guys and say a little prayer for our souls. One day soon all us will be gone and shuffled off to our eternal reward to dance and laugh and carry on until the wee hours of the morning in that great casino in the sky…

**Jim At The Santa Clara Monastery In Ohio**

# Jim's Acknowledgments

Thanks to Bill Fesi, John Dipetta, Liz Gini, Don Knight and my brother Bob for their help and stories. Also many thanks to the people I worked with in Las Vegas, the great ladies I dated and to all the people who helped me in the casino business. Thanks to Brian Carr for introducing me to Wid Bastian and Michael Beas. I'm forever indebted to Uncle Ed Pucci and Pat Ferruccio for sending me out to Vegas back in '68. Last but not least, I want to thank my mother and father for bringing up my brother Bob and myself the way they did, the right way. They are in my prayers every night. I miss them both beyond words.

Made in the USA
Lexington, KY
20 December 2017